CONCILIUM

concilium 1998/4

IS THE WORLD ENDING?

Edited by

Sean Freyne and
Nicholas Lash

SCM Press · London
Orbis Books · Maryknoll

Published by SCM Press Ltd, 9–17 St Albans Place, London N1
and by Orbis Books, Maryknoll, NY 10545

ISBN: 0 334 03050 1 (UK)
ISBN: 1 57075 190 0 (USA)

Typeset at The Spartan Press Ltd, Lymington, Hants
Printed by Biddles Ltd, Guildford and King's Lynn

Concilium Published February, April, June, October, December.

Contents

Introduction

Our title, *Is the World Ending?*, is a reminder that endings are part of the fabric of existence but that paradoxically, for many humans, the world has not yet begun. Amid the profusion of millennially-inspired literature that the advent of the year 2000 has already generated, this issue of *Concilium* attempts to present informed historical and theological discussion within a broader context of thought and action, inspired by our topic.

Is the world ending? Whose world? Some world is always ending, and some world ends when every epoch passes and every child dies. But is 'the world', the *whole* world ending, and if so, how does the ending happen? Have we done it, or is it outside our control? And if the ending of the world is near, should we regard the prospect of its ending with terror or delight?

The Jewish and Christian stories, unlike some others, have always expected a definitive ending to the world as we know it. As one ponders the implications of such an expectation, especially in the current heightened atmosphere of excitement about the year 2000, it is chastening to recall, with Aloysius Pieris, that for much of the world which counts by other calendars, and dreams other dreams, that year has no particular significance.

The year AD 2000 is only an approximate reckoning of the birth of Christ, reminding us that, unlike the natural rhythms of day and night and changing seasons, millennia, centuries and even weeks are human constructions. The symbolic association of the year 1000 was based on the expectations of 'a thousand year reign' of Christ and the martyrs, as predicted in the book of Revelation (21.4). But the year 2000 has no such resonances, despite its possible practical implications for us in this computer age, when our systems may be thrown into disarray. Nevertheless, the year 2000 is attracting expectations usually associated with the apocalyptic imagination, even in the secularized dress of 'new beginnings' in business, industry and other activities of the global market. This number of *Concilium* attempts a theological assessment of such issues.

One note that is struck by several of the contributions is the very differing perceptions that people have of such a moment of perceived transition. In line with the dualism of classic apocalyptic, those in positions of power see any radical change to the existing world order with dread, whereas the weak are buoyed with new hope by such a vision (Marcelo Barros and Aloysius Pieris). It is for this reason that Pope John Paul II has drawn on another biblical image, that of the Jubilee, as the most suitable way of giving millennial dreams a sense of reality. The radical notion of justice for the weak which the Jubilee proclaims (see Isa. 61.1–2; Luke 4.16–21) tempers the sense of future expectation with the urgency of present needs within the global family.

The year 2000 is also the beginning of a new century, and a perspective on the one just ending is the point from which responsibility for the world that we have inherited and fashioned must begin. It is a sobering experience to catalogue the traumas that our generations have experienced, so aptly and succinctly expressed by Rosemary Luling Haughton in her new book *Images for Change. The Transformation of Society*, New York 1997. She writes as follows:

> In less than one century we have experienced two world wars, several others almost as destructive, the holocaust, 'the bomb', the rise and collapse of the Soviet system, the Chinese revolution and re-revolution, the end of explicit colonialism but the neo-colonial creation of a 'third world' of economically dependent and impoverished nations, the successful control of the world economy (and therefore governments) by multi-national corporations, itself linked to massive pollution by industrial and agricultural chemicals that is endangering the earth's life-systems, the spread of AIDS, and the vast sub-culture and sub-economics of drugs. All this in three generations (3f.).

This citation might well serve as a foreword to this issue of *Concilium*. In the opening section the current context for millennial dreams is explored through the lenses of film and literature, the one a general survey of the use of apocalyptic on the screen (Michael Williams), and the other a particular view through the eye of a writer, Günter Grass. His novel, *The Rat*, has captured in a high evocative manner the nightmare scenario of the end of humanity, whose world is inherited by rats as the only form of life remaining. Yet in the very form of the novel – a dream dialogue between the author and the she-rat leaving the real outcome uncertain –

Karl-Josef Küschel finds that Grass has left us some room for hope that disaster may be averted.

The historical and theological perspectives of the next section light up the space for hope, however restricted, that Grass's novel provides. Teresa Okure's canonical reading of the Bible uncovers the connections between creation and eschatology running through the biblical story, whereas Håkan Ulfgard has highlighted both the dangers of misreading and the values of a literary-contextual approach to Revelation in uncovering the rich vein of enduring Christian hope in this work, expressed at a moment of particular crisis.

The reservation of Christian theology towards the excitement of an imminent end is not always acknowledged in popular accounts. Lewis Ayres' treatment of Augustine highlights how a classic thinker addressed the tension in Christian eschatology between present and future, whereas Damian Thompson's contribution documents the debates as to how the year 1000 was perceived in Christian circles with regard to the varying expectations that the 'thousand year reign' had engendered.

The two scientific contributions of the third section, again contrary to popular perceptions of a dominant mechanistic world-view among natural scientists, share, if for different reasons, the modesty of the theologians in answering the question that our title poses. Kenneth Hsu, invoking the Gaia principle, does not see the dangers for our planet in any natural, built-in causes, given its self-adjusting mechanisms over millennia, unlike Mars, for example. He wonders rather whether human greed might not bring about the ultimate catastrophe through the development of mass weapons of destruction. The accessible account by Andreas Albrecht and Christopher Isham of current scientific predictions about the end of the universe is equally tentative, while highlighting the sheer vastness of a universe as yet largely unexplored. 'We will just have to wait and see what will happen' is the authors' final, appropriately understated, word.

The articles which compromise the final section carry forward themes already touched on. Stephen O'Leary's informative survey of the social and psychological reasons which social scientists offer for the recurrence of millennial dreams concludes that these explanations are only partially successful. The author calls for 'a mode of millennial understanding which takes the appeal of apocalypse seriously without over-dramatizing our own historical moment'. Yet, as already alluded to, the urgency of the present moment takes on a different perspective in other contexts, as the contributions of Pieris and Barros underline.

The concluding article by Jürgen Moltmann shows how the

standpoint of Christian apocalyptic eschatology can cast a warm and encouraging light on the perennial, though often abstractly treated, question of God. If we can agree with Moltmann that the hopes and fears to which history gives rise cannot be fully realized within history, we may also learn to trust from God that the things that we fear most, namely, the ultimate nightmare of a damnation of our own making within history, may not in the end materialize.

Sean Freyne
and Nicholas Lash

I · Apocalypse in Modern Culture

Apocalypse Now

Michael E. Williams

The film *Apocalypse Now* (1979) is about the madness unleashed by the war in Viet Nam, and not about the coming of the kingdom. It is one of many films that express a feeling common to a generation which has been confronted with man's inhumanity to man. Events in the Soviet and Nazi death camps, massacres in Cambodia and Rwanda, can prompt our imagination to depict even greater horrors and to fear the collapse of civilization and the end of the world. In these circumstances films like *The Beast from 20,000 Fathoms* (1953), *Earthquake* (1974), *Towering Inferno* (1974), *The Omen* (1976), *Jurassic Park* (1993) are only too plausible; they fascinate us because they reflect our basic insecurity. A somewhat similar attraction is exercised by the growing number of religious movements and sects that fasten on to this fear of the end of the world. The prognostications of science do not present us with sufficient reasons for living, and people turn to those religions that preach a way of life that leads to salvation. This usually involves a leader who will deliver us from the impending disaster at some definite date in the future.

Apocalyptic language comes easily to people today, because it is so refreshingly different from the technical and detached way in which disturbing events are announced by popular science. Cool objective statements cannot convey the emotion and fear that is evoked in our hearts when we are told about the end to which the material world is hastening. Because it concerns the fate of the human race, the full reality of the news we receive lies beyond technology's powers of measurement. It is because mere information is not enough that we have recourse to metaphor.[1] However, the scope of this metaphorical language has to be understood with care. We must not downgrade and falsify it by treating it as if it were no more than literal truth. It is much richer and fuller. To interpret the apocalyptic literally is to distort it. Moreover, such language is provoked by expectations of the future. It is not primarily concerned with the future as future, since this has not yet taken place. It is about our hopes and fears for the future. It is about a present state of mind rather than the advance reporting of an event that is yet to come. So, when we speak of the end of the world, we are not restricting the word 'end' to the future. We are also talking about the present. End has to do with purpose and meaning. It is a matter of teleology. The point at issue in apocalyptic is the purpose and meaning of the world we live in here and now, a purpose or end that is already operating, although not yet fully revealed or accomplished.

This gives relevance to the matter under discussion, since most people, including those in the film industry and their audiences, are much more interested in their everyday joys and sorrows than in events that might or might not happen in the distant future.

The specificity of film

It is in this context that we have to examine film. Films vary enormously in style and quality, and film-makers are motivated in diverse ways and have different ideals. But we have to consider film as such. What specific qualities characterize it as a medium, and how is it related to the apocalyptic?

First of all, cinema is one of the mass media. Films appeal to all classes and all ages. Unlike other art forms, one sometimes has to deter rather than encourage children and adolescents from indulging too much in film-going. Since the language of cinema is primarily visual, it has a potentially world-wide audience, and many films can be dubbed or subtitled with little loss to their intelligibility. Since the advent of TV and the video an even larger distribution is possible.

Secondly, every picture tells a story. If one is going to talk about a theology of cinema, then it will have to be a narrative theology. A good story, because it has a beginning, a middle and an end, attracts and holds people's attention and, as a rule, at least some of the story remains in the memory. Despite their great diversity, there are certain common factors to be found in the many tales that have been told down the ages. There are recurring myths. Many North American 'Westerns' are remakes of Homer, and the ancient Greek myths reappear in Japanese cinema. Stories are one of the easiest ways of getting across ideas. In his introduction to the film *Alphaville* (1965), the French director, J. L. Godard, said, 'Sometimes reality is too complex for oral communication, but myth embodies it in a form which enables it to spread all over the world.'

Thirdly, although cinema is mainly a visual art, it has the ability to go beyond vision and reach the inmost feelings and sensibilities of the spectator. The early Soviet film-makers realized this, and saw the possibilities in cinema for propaganda among the illiterate masses. V. Pudovkin, the Russian director, said, 'Film is the greatest teacher, because it teaches not only through the brain, but through the whole body.' How does this happen? We may go to the cinema alone or with companions, but once we have bought our ticket and settled in our seat, the lights are dimmed and we are in the dark and subject to a partial sensory deprivation, so that the screen can take over and draw us into another world.[2] Seeing a film in a darkened cinema is not like watching television or a video at home. We are more free. There are no distractions, nor do our instinctive reactions need to be stifled because of the presence of watchful others. There is no eye contact with our neighbour. In the most successful films the spectator is not merely a passive observer but becomes absorbed and participates in what is happening on the screen. We can be provoked into love or hatred, we can laugh or weep in our own particular way. Personal and private memories can be stirred. We can identify with the characters and share in their moral dilemmas and choices. This total absorption into something other than everyday life bears some resemblance to the effect that great preachers in the past had on their congregations. During a good film we do not have to consult our watch. Clock-time does not matter, because the film-maker constructs his own time. The author is the one who determines the sequence in which events are shown, who marshals them in a different order from the chronological. *Montage* places together two disparate images so that they can combine to make a new concept. They become related by association. Flash-backs and flash-forwards destroy the conventional sequence of past, present and future. We are taken into another world where time and space have different dimensions. Seeing a film in these conditions is a total experience, and we can come out of the cinema refreshed in spirit with a renewed outlook on life, even if this change only lasts a short time.

Film and the future

As the early film-makers began to appreciate the possibilities of this powerful medium, so there emerged broadly speaking, two styles or tendencies: the fantastic and the real.[3] George Méliès in *Le Voyage dans la Lune* (1902) saw a way of using film to show the absurd, the fantastic, the comic. He is the true parent of Chaplin, Keaton, Cantinflas, Benny Hill

and other great comics, and also of the impossible adventures of James
Bond and the special effects of a Steven Spielberg film. This is the kind of
film that easily lends itself to depicting the end of the world, either the end
of a particular world as in *Independence Day* (1996), or of a whole galaxy as
in *Star Wars* (1977). The cinema is able to allow full rein to the
imagination, and because it is a visual medium it can give an air of
verisimilitude to extraordinary and improbable events. Such films can
amuse, entertain and illustrate the wildest dreams and speculations of
science. Many of them are escapist and good entertainment, but little else.
Sometimes, however, there is a deeper meaning, and they betray an
anxiety and concern about the future. *Dr Strangelove – or How I Learned
to Stop Worrying and Love the Bomb* (1964) is a variation on the theme of
the 'mad scientist', but below the surface there is a thinly disguised fear
that the human race, either deliberately or through negligence, might
unleash powers that it is unable to control. When confronted with films of
an apocalyptic kind involving the destruction of worlds and powers
superior to humankind, one has to use discernment and not be carried
away by the imagery or ingenuity of the latest Hollywood techniques. Just
as excessive literalism is a trap into which the reader of the Bible can fall, so
the language of film can have deeper resonances than those which flash
spectacularly before our eyes on the screen. Interest in 'special effects' can
distract us from the serious questions that are present in the text.

Some of these films deal with visitors to earth from another planet,
either by means of futuristic spaceships (*Close Encounters of the Third
Kind*, 1977; *ET*, 1982) or by strange appearances from apparently
nowhere (*Hombre Mirando al Sudeste*, 1986). Astronauts make journeys
into outer space and reach planets where mysterious forces are at work
(*Solaris*, 1972). The story-line often makes use of the myth of the quest
or journey (*2001 – A Space Odyssey*, 1968) and the conflict between good
and evil (*Star Wars*, 1977). The question is posed whether man is the
only intelligent being in the universe. Although no reference is made to
any organized religious belief or practice, nevertheless religious questions are raised. Among these fantasy films there are one or two that
deserve special mention, because they are trying to discover what it really
means to be human; but they pose their questions in a sensitive manner
and not in the threatening way of a religious enthusiast who knows the
answers. They respect that anxious curiosity which is characteristic of
many in our contemporary society.[4] *Bladerunner* (1982), *The Terminator*
(1984), *Terminator 2 – Judgment Day* (1991) deal with highly sophisticated computers, artificial intelligences.[5] Unlike the machines in *Star
Wars* and *2001*, Artoo Detoo and HAL, the Cyborgs and Replicants are

clothed in human flesh and appear to be indistinguishable from 'real' human beings. They are creations of man but are no longer under human control. They were built as robots to serve humankind, but have revolted and are now our enemy. Their existence calls attention to the problem of human responsibility, and the film contains warnings of the catastrophe that can come from a misuse of our intelligence. The human race has to be saved from itself. The opening scene of the film *The Terminator* is violent, but not gratuitously so, since it could be taken as a visual presentation of a passage from one of the Old Testament prophets, Jeremiah or Malachi. The crushing of human skulls might be a scene from Cambodia in the days of Pol Pot with echoes of Golgotha, the place of the skull. Just as the prophets threaten God's judgment, so *Terminator 2* has as its secondary title *Judgment Day*. In Old Testament times the people of Israel, although brought out of exile and restored, ceased to trust in God; today the human race is using its God-given wealth and technology to produce even more horrid weapons of destruction. The laying waste of the planet is not merely due to an outside cause; it is suggested that the blame is ultimately attributable in some way to the human race. Knowledge has been pursued with too little reference to responsibility. The Cyborgs appear on earth in a perfect bodily form and are superior to us in so far as they are able to assume different likenesses and mimic other human beings. They can even have memories implanted in them from elsewhere. However, they are not able to experience the whole range of human emotions. They feel no reluctance at killing other members of the race to which they are supposed to belong, and they are completely mystified as to why human beings cry. Much of this is conveyed visually, and it is the imagination that prompts our mind to pose serious philosophical and theological questions about human freedom and destiny. Admittedly not everybody who sees the film for the first time will understand it in this way, but a careful consideration of the text and a knowledge of the author James Cameron will confirm the basic seriousness of the work.

A further point: precisely because it is a film, the plot can revolve round an ingenious use of time. On the screen the future can be visualized in as realistic a way as the present, so that it is difficult to distinguish between the two. This happens with us in everyday life when our fear of the future is as vivid and influential on our actions as what is actually happening to us in the present. These super-machine intelligences, working from a knowledge and experience of the future, intervene in the present (which they see as past), and they send a 'terminator' to prevent and undo the future. The terminator sets out to kill a young woman and so prevent her becoming a mother and generating the son who is to engineer the ultimate downfall of the Cyborgs. This is more than an ingenious use of a scientific theory of relativity. It is also asking the question whether it is possible to alter our future by undoing the past. One of the messages of the film would seem to be that the future is not fixed. Judgment Day is not so much in the future as now, in the present. There is something here that is reminiscent of St Paul's regarding the early Christians as those 'upon whom the ends of the ages have come' (I Cor. 10.11).[6]

It is to be noted that despite the futuristic overtones, these films are situated in a recognizably human landscape. There are city scenes with offices, board meetings, super-automobiles, personal computers as well as families and children. This background has its parallel in the way the Italian masters showed the countryside of Tuscany and Umbria in their religious paintings of the time of Christ. The story may be marvellous and incredible, but it is bound up with the actual world we know and inhabit. However, there is no mention of religion in the conventional sense: church going, worship, prayer, gods. But we must remember that the mere choice of a religious subject, like Samson and Delilah or David and Bathsheba, does not necessarily herald a film with religious significance. A seemingly secular subject need not be irreligious. Just as apocalyptic literature can carry a deeper spiritual meaning by stressing imaginatively a vision of an earthly catastrophe, so film working on our senses and imagination can turn the mind to deeper considerations. Such an assessment of science-fiction films is not shared by all critics. Very often they judge according to the special effects: the violence, the shocks to the senses, the twists and surprises that are produced on our jaded palates, the improbable feats of the superstar.[7] But this is a very superficial view, as it does not touch on the meaning of the film. This sort of criticism is equivalent to an over-literal reading of apocalyptic passages in the Bible, where beasts and monsters and signs in the sky are given too much attention and mistaken for the realities they are meant to represent. Perception, ability to read the signs of the times, is required on the part of the critic as well as the believer. Unfortunately many believers today are unaware and insensitive to the presence of the sacred within the secular, and so are incapable of feeding the spiritual hunger that is latent in many of the dreams and fantasies of science fiction.[8]

The sacred revealed in the everyday

The ability of film to present the fantastic and inspire the imagination to probe questions concerning the destiny of the human race with greater feeling and urgency has been a characteristic of many films coming from Hollywood over the last forty years.[9] But ultimate questions have been posed by the camera in other ways and in other places. In their first brief fifty-second attempts at cinematography the brothers Lumière in *La Sortie des usines Lumière à Lyon* (1895) showed that the camera could call attention to everyday events and pick up things that the human eye had overlooked. The camera has taught us that the material world is more wonderful than appears at first sight. The photographic lens is able to show us 'nature caught in the act'. In this, film follows the tradition of Western European painting. Luca Signorelli's frescoes of zooming fixed-wing angels and devils in Orvieto cathedral, and Michelangelo's Last Judgment with its gravity-free human figures floating in a planet-blue sky have something of the cosmic qualities of science-fiction Armageddon. But in paint one can also express the human person and reveal through the face and gesture something of the spirit that is present in the body. The great portrait painters like Velazquez have shown us something of the dignity of humankind. Remarkably similar effects have been achieved in films like Dreyer's *The Passion of Joan of Arc* (1928) and Bresson's *Diary of a Country Priest* (1950), where through the human face the camera reveals things of the spirit. The Italian cinema, from De Sica's *Ladri di Biciclette* (1948) to Tornatore's *Cinema Paradiso* (1988), shows us the significance of everyday things, while the works of Ingmar Bergman and his cameraman Sven Nukvist can lead us 'through a glass darkly', through the lives of ordinary worried people to a deeper reality. It was Pasolini, another portraitist of the human race, who once remarked 'tutto é sacro'. The sacred cannot by-pass the material world. This helps to put the apocalyptic in the wider context of a sacramental view of reality. In the last analysis the heart of the Christian message is to be found in the life, death and resurrection of Jesus, and it is the Christ of the Gospels, the man of Nazareth, who will come again in glory.

It is not possible to make a film about the end of the world or about the coming of the kingdom. These are truths beyond human experience in this age. But it is possible to portray human fears and hopes which are affecting contemporary society and which may be indications of the ultimate direction of human endeavour.

Notes

1. The limitations of the claims of science and the role of belief and credulity among scientists are discussed at length in Mary Midgley's 1990 Gifford Lectures, *Science as Salvation. A Modern Myth and its Meaning*, London and New York 1992.

2. It is said that Wittgenstein in his Cambridge days used to go to the Arts Cinema, sit in the front row, and let the film sweep over him as if immersed in a bath.

3. This distinction between Mélies and Lumière is noted by Michael Bird, 'Film as Hierophany', in J. R. May and M. Bird, *Religion in Film*, University of Tennessee, Knoxville 1982.

4. Unfortunately some religious minded believers are inclined to consider film from too narrow a perspective as a weapon of propaganda, rather than allowing it to do its own work and influence the spectator in its own subtle way.

5. For a full treatment of these films see C. Marsh and G. W. Ortiz (eds), *Movies and Meaning. Explorations in Theology & Film*, Oxford 1997, especially the chapter on *The Terminator* by Gaye Ortiz and Maggie Roux.

6. Frank Kermode, *The Sense of an Ending*, Oxford and New York 1967, treats of an apocalyptic mode of thinking and its relation to literary fiction. Perhaps Scotus provides us with a theological application of the future acting retrospectively in the present. He speaks of the merits of Christ preserving his mother from sin. In her case, uniquely, his grace forestalled any contraction of original sin.

7. The otherwise admirable British Film Institute publication, *The Terminator*, by Sean French, 1996, falls into this trap.

8. This is related to such matters as the Western world's loss of a sense of wholeness. See N. Lash, *The Beginning and End of 'Religion'*, Cambridge 1996.

9. J. W. Martin and C. E. Ostwalt Jr (eds), *Screening the Sacred*, San Francisco 1995.

The Nightmare of the End of Humankind

The apocalypse in the work of Günter Grass

Karl-Josef Kuschel

None of the great contemporary German authors with an international reputation has been so radically preoccupied with the theme of the threat to creation and the end of the world as Günter Grass. His novel *The Rat* appeared in 1986, and the burning wound which it has inflicted on the European literary consciousness can still be felt. Here I interpret this novel as a paradigm of the possibilities that a writer has today in struggling with the problem of giving the topic of the apocalypse vivid poetic form.

I. The Enlightenment has failed

In a dream of the narrator, the reader of *The Rat* is shown the possibility that the self-destruction of humankind has already taken place and that after this end of the human period, only rats have survived. Grass presents world theatre – though with the difference that the curtain already seems to have fallen on the last act of the drama of humankind. For the narrator, circling the earth in a space capsule, surveys the total devastation of the earth and what life is still left on an earth devoid of human beings. I do not want to go into the details of the complex strands of action here; I want to work out the basic structure and see how this author has dealt with the question of hope in a hopeless time. If I have deciphered the basic structure rightly, in this novel we have calculated oscillation between reality and possibility, reality and dream, fact and fate.

On the one hand there is the hard confrontation with the possibility that humankind will bring nuclear destruction upon itself. The novel offers every possible argument in favour of this possibility: the forests are being allowed to die, there is the madness of nuclear over-armament – fed by a notion of security which is guaranteed by the 'balance of terror'; divestment of the self by the delegation of responsibility to apparatuses; the inability to learn from former catastrophes and really to take seriously the Enlightenment ideal of the 'education of the human race' to be humane. This humane scepticism, indeed the conviction that the Enlightenment has failed, which glimmers throughout the novel, is given most concentrated expression in one of its key poems:

Our intention was that men should learn
little by little
to handle not only knife and fork
but one another as well, and reason too,
that omnipotent can opener.

That once educated, the human race should freely,
yes, freely, determine its destiny and free from its shackles
learn to guide nature cautiously,
as cautiously as possible,
away from chaos.

That in the course of its education the human race
would cultivate the virtue of eating with a spoon
and diligently practise the use of the subjunctive and tolerance,
difficult as this may be
among brothers.

A special lesson enjoined us
to watch over the sleep of reason
to domesticate all dream animals until
grown docile they eat out of the hand
of the Enlightenment.

Halfway enlightened, the human race
ceased to play crazily, aimlessly in the primordial muck
and began to wash systematically.
Acquired hygiene spoke plainly:
Woe to the dirty.

Once our education claimed to be advanced,
knowledge was declared to be power and

no longer confined to paper.
The Enlightened cried:
Woe to the ignorant!

When finally violence, all reason to the contrary,
could not be banished from the world,
the human race taught itself mutual deterrence.
Thus it learned to keep the peace until some unenlightened
accident happened.

Then at last the education of the human race
was virtually complete. A great light
illumined every corner. Too bad that afterward
it grew so dark that no one
could find his school.[1]

In this poem Grass draws a line of decadence through the history of culture. It goes through the following stages: primal mud (nature) – reason (knowledge) – power (violence) – mutual deterrent – atomic annihilation. Along this line the course of humankind can be described only as going 'in the wrong direction'. Something has gone wrong: there is something wrong with creation generally. But a collective blindness prevents people from 'asking any longer where, what and when a mistake was made'. Nor does anyone 'ask about guilt or guilty parties'. This is expressed very vividly in another poem from the novel:

Something must be wrong
I don't know what, the direction maybe.
Some mistake, but what, has been made
but when and where wrong
especially as everything's been running like clockwork,
though in a direction
which signs demonstrate to be wrong.

Now we are looking for the source of error.
Frantically looking for it outside ourselves,
Until someone says we,
we could all of us, just for the sake of argument, be
the source of error, yes,
it could be you or you or you.
We don't mean it personally.

Each gives the next man precedence.
While everything is running like clockwork

in the wrong direction,
which even if it's wrong is said to be
the only one, men greet
each other with the cry:
I am the source of error, you too?

Seldom had there been such consensus.
No one asks any longer where what and when
a mistake was made.
Nor does anyone ask about
guilt or guilty parties.

For after all we know that each of us,
contentedly as never before we all run
in the wrong direction, follow the signs,
hoping that they're wrong
and that we're saved again.[2]

There is no perception that the direction is wrong. It is drowned out by
the naive hope that we will be 'saved again'.

II. Rats take over from human beings

The novel depicts this syndrome of blindness, repression and naive
temporizing better than any other in the German literature of the 1980s.
Its consequences are illustrated vividly: human beings themselves put an
end to their own position in the cosmos. And because this is the case, no
human being stands at the centre of the novel but an animal, the most
cunning and adaptable in the history of evolution. The rat becomes
the counterpart of human beings. And this rat is made to utter all
the contempt for humankind which human beings have themselves
deserved:

Finished! she says. You people used to be, you're has-beens, a
remembered delusion. Never again will you set dates. All your prospects wiped out. You're washed up. Completely. It was high time.[3]

So it is only consistent that even the narrator in the dream does not
exclude the possibility of finally having to take leave. A poem is
deliberately put at the beginning of the novel which once again – as the
author explains in a personal comment – 'in a love for life, lists everything
that gives joy, from the small things to the ideas which human beings
have'.[4] So it is a farewell poem, which proves all the more painful, the

more one conjures up once more these 'things' which have come to be
loved.

I dreamed I had to take leave
of all the things that have surrounded me
and cast their shadows: all those possessive
pronouns. Leave of the inventory, that list
of found objects. Leave
of cloying scents
and smells that keep me awake,
of the sweet, the bitter,
the intrinsically sour,
and the hot pungency of peppercorns.
Leave of time's tick tock, of Monday's irritation,
of Wednesday's shabby gains, of Sunday's
bitchiness, once boredom sits down to table.
Leave of all deadliness, of everything due
to come due.

I dreamed I had to take leave of all
ideas, whether born quick or still, of the meaning
that looks for the meaning behind the meaning,
and of hope, that long-distance runner. Leave of the compound
    interest
of pent-up rage, of the proceeds of accumulated dreams,
of everything that's written on paper and recalls metaphor, when horse
    and
rider become a monument. Leave
of all the images that man has made for himself.
Leave of songs, of rhymed misery,
of interwoven voices, of six-choired jubilation,
of instrumental enthusiasm,
of God and Bach.[5]

Taking leave, then, of 'hope, that long-distance runner'. Taking leave of
'ideas of meaning'. Literally? But there is a counter-current in this novel
which prevents the dream which it outlines from becoming a complete
nightmare. For the novel is written as a duel in words between the
narrator and the She-rat. It is certainly not simply to be 'trivialized' as a
dream (as a dream it still remains a possible reality); at the same time the
narrator is speaking against the She-rat. Both narrative positions (those
of the narrator and the She-rat) are linked as dreams. To begin with, for

the narrator the She-rat and her stories are dreams; later the narrator becomes the product of the She-rat's dream. The conclusion leaves it open who is dreaming whom. In this way reality becomes shaky, though there is always a chronological distance between fact and fate. This leaves scope for hope – above all for the reader.

III. Whither literature, if there is no future?

There had been preparations for the anthropological and political scepticism which underlie this novel in Grass's work. His tone had still been confident in his 1980 book *Headbirths, or The Germans are Dying Out.* The book ended with the invitation to the readers readily to take upon themselves the burden of existence, and offered Camus' interpretation of the myth of Sisyphus as a reason. But as early as 1982 a shift became evident in the thinking of the author, who formerly had been even involved in party politics, though in his *Tagebuch einer Schnecke* (1972) he had already shattered the socialist utopian hopes with concrete political experiences. In 1982 Grass gave a speech when he was awarded the international Antonio Feltrinelli Prize in Rome. And in this speech for the first time he made quite clear what the caesura is with which literature is confronted in our time.

Hitherto, Grass argued, literature had been able to look back on a proud history of victories: 'Victories of the book over the censor, the poet over the potentates.' Literature had always been sure of an ally, however dirty things had got: the future. Silone and Moravia, Brecht and Döblin, had survived Fascism, just as Isaak Babel and Ossip Mandelstam had survived Stalinism. For according to Grass literature had always had 'stamina'. It had been able to take the long-term view, certain of its influence, even if it took decades and sometimes even centuries for the echo of words and sentences, poems and theses, to develop. Indeed this advantage of time had made the poorest writers rich. It had been impossible to stifle them even in 'the most resistent present'. Writers had been imprisoned, beaten or exiled, but in the end 'the book and with it the word' had always triumphed.

But today things looked different. How could 'the future' still be literature's ally if there was no future for humankind? Grass remarked:

For with the threat that the future will be lost to humankind, the 'immortality of literature' which hitherto was assured has now degenerated into an unreal claim. People are already talking of the throwaway poem. The book, that permanent object, is beginning to resemble a disposable bottle. Even before it is decided whether we still have a future, people are no longer taking any account of the future. The same hybris which enables human beings to destroy themselves, now threatens, before that can be done, to darken the human spirit, to quench the human dream of a better future and to make any utopia – including Ernst Bloch's *Principle of Hope* – ridiculous.[6]

What is the way out? Or, to ask a more modest question, precisely what can be done? For Grass the answer was already clear in 1982: human beings must be prepared to practice renunciation over their discoveries, to disarm in ecological and military terms 'to the point of nakedness'.

Can human beings succeed in showing restraint? Are these beings, endowed with reason, godlike in their creativity, and also capable of inventing their total annihilation, capable of saying no to their inventions? Are they ready to exercise restraint towards what is humanly possible and to be modest towards the remains of a destroyed nature? And a last question. Do we want to do what we could do: feed one another until hunger is only a legend, a bad story of 'once upon a time'?

The answers to these questions are overdue. And I cannot give them. But in my perplexity I nevertheless know that the future will be possible again only if we find an answer and do what we ought to do as guests on this globe of nature, by no longer making one another anxious, by relieving one another of anxiety, by disarming to the point of nakedness.[7]

The author's 'perplexity' intensified further during the 1980s, and *The Rat* is an expression of it. Above all in the face of the failure of the disarmament negotiations between the great powers in the 1980s, Grass gave up hope that human beings could really be ready to say no to its inventions in an act of renunciation, organize society globally in such a way that hunger disappeared, and shape their relationship to nature in such a way that they understood themselves anew as 'guests on this globe of nature'.

IV. Struggling with the possibility of hope

Moreover the end of *The Rat* is all one struggle with the possibility of hope. On the last three pages there is a gripping song of hope which could be the counterpart to the song of farewell with which the novel opens. Moreover the first lines of both songs are diametrically opposed: the first poem began 'I dreamed I had to take leave', and now the poem begins with the line 'I dreamed that I could take hope'. This hope is spelt out strophe by strophe. It would almost be infectious, were it not for the laughter of the She-rat, which shows up such hope as self-deception.

I dreamed that I could take hope,
barely a crumb or whatever is left
on plates eaten clean, and hope that something,
not an idea, more like an accident,
supposedly friendly, was on its way,
unobstructed by frontiers,
that it was spreading, contagious,
a salutary plague.

I dreamed that I could hope again
for winter apples, Martinmas goose,
strawberries year after year,
for my sons' incipient baldness,
my daughters' green, my grandchildren's postcard greetings,
for advances and compound interest, as though mankind
had unlimited credit again.

I dreamed that hope was permissible
and looked for words to justify it,
dreaming to justify my hope.
So I tried, I said good,
new, small hope. First cautious,
then sudden, I thought. I called it
treacherous, begged it to have mercy on us.
The last hope I dreamed
was consumptive.

I dreamed: A last hope is permissible;
there's sympathy and understanding.
People leave their ignition keys lying around,
They trust one another and leave their doors unlocked.
My hope did not deceive me;
no one ate his bread unshared; except that the merriment
I had hoped for, though all-embracing, was not
our kind of merriment: rats were laughing at us
when the very last hope was forfeit.

But the narrator has not yet confessed defeat; he still contends with the She-rat over this, his 'last hope'. For despite all the rattish laughter, the narrator wants to maintain a perspective. And so the book ends at least with a hypothesis:

> Only assuming that we humans are still . . .
> All right. Let's assume
> . . . but this time let us live for one another and peacefully, do you hear, gently and lovingly, as nature made us.
> A beautiful dream, said the She-rat, before dissolving.[9]

So what is the ultimate aim of this book? Historical fatalism and a radical renunciation of the Enlightenment? Is the destruction of humankind to some degree unstoppable? Is it coming like an apocalyptic horror which human beings can no longer influence? In his 'personal interpretations' of the novel Grass is as divided as in the overall conception of it.[10] On the one hand he depicts human beings in his book as defeated. For him as a narrator 'the arguments for the human position' to be made against the She-rat are 'bankrupt'. Unfortunately the She-rat is more convincing. So his book is a 'catastrophic book at a catastrophic time'; it corresponds to 'our time, our situation', but he, Grass, is attempting to present the whole 'not in a melancholy way' but with his own means, including all the 'comedy' that there is in such a desperate situation. His book is not meant to be 'a book to fake hope, but to communicate insight, to convey terror'. For if people again want to have reason to hope, insight into and fear about the situation into which 'we' have got ourselves are indispensable presuppositions.

Such remarks already show that the last point of refuge of the argument in this book is the prevention of catastrophe. On the other hand, Grass thinks it very important to note that his novel is not an apocalyptic book in the classical sense. An 'apocalypse in the sense of that of John on Patmos' would mean the acceptance of a 'dark fate' imposed on us, which human beings cannot change. So his novel is 'not a book with seven seals'. The threat that is there is all 'human work'; including the 'self-destruction of the human race'. So it could also be 'only human work' if we wanted to avert it. As Grass points out: 'There is no excuse. We cannot say that the fate is imposed from above so that we cannot escape it. We could escape it if we acted against it.'

Thus acting against it might have been the author's ultimate motivation in writing this novel. There is an insistence on political action, though this now no longer stems from a political vision but from a desperate comedy. Grass's book still works by a poetics of catharsis – to some degree in a last act of trust in the Enlightenment: the possible reality of human self-destruction is meant to terrify and thus produce a reverse effect. At any rate readers are not to see their political fatalism confirmed by this novel and react to the apocalyptic maxim with the attitude that destruction can come – and the sooner, the better. So Grass is writing from a basic attitude of doubt which is not greater only because not to write would only accelerate the process of destruction and further the forces which are indifferent as to whether the world goes to the devil. The author himself points in this direction when, alluding to his poem, 'I dreamed I had to take leave', he remarks:

This poem, in a love for life, lists everything that gives joy, from the small things to the ideas which human beings have. That shows that I am very attached to life and do not know anything better than living. And I also attempt to make something of this possibility of living consciously – with the means that I have. In writing *The Rat* it was not my concern to write a sinister book about destruction. There are very comic passages in this book, and I think that that is also conveyed to the reader. Because comedy, desperate comedy, is often also the most precise expression of despair. It goes with the book.[11]

Translated by John Bowden

Notes

1. Günter Grass, *The Rat*, translated by Ralph Manheim, Secker and Warburg 1987, 132.
2. Ibid., 161f.
3. Ibid., 3.
4. G. Grass, 'Mir träumte, ich müsste Abschied nehmen. Gespräch mit B. Pinkerneil', in *Werkausgabe in 10 Bänden*, ed. V. Neuhaus, X, *Gespräche*, Darmstadt and Neuwied 1987, 342–58: 350.
5. Grass, *The Rat* (n. 1), 79f.
6. G. Grass, 'Der Vernichtung der Menschheit hat begonnen. Rede zur Verleihung des Internationalen Antonio-Feltrinelli-Preises für erzählende Prosa in Rom (November 1982)', in *Werkausgabe* (n. 4), IX, *Essays, Reden, Briefe, Kommentare*, 830–3: 831f.
7. Ibid., 833.
8. Grass, *The Rat* (n. 1), 356f.
9. Ibid., 358.
10. The following quotations are taken from the conversation between G. Grass and B. Pinkerneil.
11. Grass, 'Mir träumte' (n. 4), 350.

II · Biblical and Historical Reflections

From Genesis to Revelation: Apocalyptic in Biblical Faith

Teresa Okure

Biblical apocalyptic is a mysterious phenomenon. The mystery surrounds its origin, nature, purpose, language and relation to prophecy. Of particular interest is its bearing on human history in terms of actual events and time projections. Efforts have been made in the past and the present to interpret the Book of Revelation, for instance, within the confines of actual historical events or to divide history into its time frames.[1]

This study leaves aside issues such as those highlighted above. It seeks mainly to appraise the central message of apocalyptic within the context of biblical history and faith. What, in biblical faith and view of the world, makes apocalyptic message comprehensible, and, perhaps, even necessary? The rationale for this approach is the canonical shape of the Bible itself which begins with Genesis and ends with Revelation. Brevard Childs long ago pointed out that the canonical shape of the Bible has a message of its own.[2] The nature of this message and its relevance for today's Christian constitute our major concern.

To situate our focus better, here are four observations. First, apocalyptic is an end-time phenomenon: it emerges from an end-time and generally narrates revelatory visions of what will happen at the end-time on a cosmic scale.[3] Because it is difficult to visualize such an end, apocalyptic uses fantastic and esoteric language and symbols to portray it. Whether the visionary actually sees what is described or makes it up in an effort to express the inexpressible is not the issue here. The vivid portrayal is an act of faith, that what is described will surely happen (cf. Rev. 22.5).

Secondly, apocalyptic revelation, like prophecy, claims God (or God in Christ) as its author and guarantor. Rev. 22.20 states this vividly. Some scholars see apocalyptic as an inferior form of prophecy, or what is left when prophecy runs out. While prophecy is essentially a message of salvation for the present, addressed orally to a particular audience, apocalyptic is mainly a vision shown to the recipient to write down. Its message carries a threat of what will happen if its warnings are not heeded. Unlike prophecy, it assumes that its warnings will be ignored. Hence it carries its threat to the end by vividly portraying scenes where it is actualized (e.g., Revelation 5–8).

Thirdly, apocalyptic emerges in times of persecution and crises, or is connected with persecution yet to come (e.g., Mark 13 and parallels). It carries a message of hope for those undergoing persecution for God's cause, in an effort to strengthen them to endure to the end.

Fourthly, and most importantly, apocalyptic focusses on the destruction of evil, not philosophical and theological, but as it exists concretely in human hearts and in this world's systems: political, economic, religious, racial, social, cultural and moral, with their architects, beasts and false prophets. Recognition of the existence of evil in all its forms and belief in its final eradication may be said to constitute the Leitmotif of apocalyptic.

The biblical perspective accepts the message of the Bible as divine revelation. This revelation begins with the creation of 'heaven and earth' (Gen. 1.1–2.4; esp. 2.1), and ends with the creation of 'a new heaven and a new earth' (Rev. 21–22; esp. 21.1). It proclaims God's presence and action in history to ensure the fulfilment of the divine plan against the onslaught of evil. Viewed in this light, apocalyptic faith permeates the entire Bible.[4] A study of apocalyptic in biblical perspective invites one to identify why this is so. The central argument of the study is that biblical faith in God and its doctrine of creation hold the key for understanding the apocalyptic message which finds its summit in the Book of Revelation.

Briefly stated, the thesis of apocalyptic faith is as follows. God created the world very good. Through the deceit of the serpent/Satan (Gen. 3.1–4), evil entered the world, brought sin and death to humans and decay to creation. In Rev. 12.19 this enemy of God, humanity and creation is called 'the dragon, the primeval serpent, . . . the devil or Satan'. God's immediate response was to promise humanity victory over the serpent/Satan (Gen. 3.15). From then on, the history of humanity in biblical perspective unfolds as a continuous combat between those who obey God and those who follow evil. Evil attacks God's followers, especially in the form of religious persecution, even within the same religious affiliation (e.g., Jeremiah pitted against the entire nation, Jer. 1.18–19). Apocalyptic faith believes and declares that this combat will have an end in the final destruction of evil. Jesus' parable of the wheat and the darnel (Matt. 13.24–30) may shed light on this.

Seen within the entire biblical spectrum, belief in God's victory over Satan, sin and death is not peculiar to apocalyptic faith; it is the soul of biblical faith. Jeremiah spoke of it in terms of 'a new covenant' (31.31–34). The concept of the 'new heaven(s) and new earth' itself was first enunciated by Trito-Isaiah (65.17). For Paul, not only human beings but the entire creation will benefit from God's final victory in Christ, by being set free from its bondage to decay (Rom. 8.19–21). Biblical history has an inbuilt future perspective, whether this be in terms of the messianic expectation, the Parousia or the apocalyptic faith of Revelation.

Testing the thesis: Genesis 3 and Rev. 12.1–17

For practical purposes, we limit our testing of the above thesis to a thematic study of Genesis 3 and Revelation 12, within their respective contexts. In the first passage, the serpent/Satan tempts humanity to disobey God and thus succeeds, against God's will (cf. Wisdom 2.23–24), in bringing sin and death into the world (Gen. 3.1–7, 18–19). God then promises to put a two-fold enmity between the serpent and the woman, his offspring and her offspring. The offspring or the woman, depending on whether one follows the Massoretic Text or the Vulgate, will crush the head of the serpent, who will resort to striking at his or her heel. The establishment of this enmity between them is God's action, hence the possibility of its failing is ruled out.

In this passage, God stands over against the situation of sin and death by promising victory to humanity through the woman. He constitutes the woman and her offspring as the divine instrument for this victory. At key moments of biblical history, one encounters women who served as God's instruments of victory over evil. The Egyptian midwives, Shiphrah and Puah (Exod. 1.15–21); Moses' mother, sister and Pharaoh's daughter (Exod. 2.1–10), formed a coalition against death-dealing forces and thus saved the life of their offspring Moses. Through him God brought about the liberation of Israel from slavery and extinction. In Isa. 7.14, 'the maiden with child' serves as God's sign that the political threat to Judah posed by Damascus and Samaria is doomed to fail.

The decisive victory of the woman and her offspring over the serpent/Satan is given in Rev. 12.1–17. This scene in many ways evokes, perhaps deliberately, the scene in Gen. 3.15–16. These are the key motifs common to both passages:

- the woman (Gen. 3.1, 2, 4, 6, 12, 13, 15, 16; Rev. 12.1, 5, 6, 14, 15).
- the serpent as deceiver (Gen. 3.1–4; Rev. 12.9).
- pain in childbearing (Gen. 3.16; Rev. 12.2).
- enmity between the woman/her seed and Satan/his followers (Gen. 3.15; Rev. 12.4–6, 13–17; the 'third of the sky' dragged to the earth by the dragon's tail in Rev. 12.4 symbolizes the fallen angels, Satan's offspring, Rev. 12.9).
- fruitless attempt of Satan to crush the woman and her seed (Gen. 3.15; Rev. 12.4b–6, 13–17).
- the woman, as 'mother': of all the living (Gen. 3.20) or of the male child and all who obey God's commandment and bear witness to Jesus (Rev. 12.5, 13, 17).
- the final defeat of Satan, victory to God who effects it, and to the woman and her seed, on whose behalf he effects it (Gen. 3.15; Rev. 12.10–12).

Revelation 12.1 portrays the woman in cosmic majesty, clothed with the sun, standing on the moon, but in labour pains. She and her child are vulnerable to the attacks of the dragon/Satan; but God comes to their rescue: the child is snatched up to God in heaven, from where Satan and his angels have just been flung out (12.7–8), and a place is prepared for the woman beyond Satan's reach (12.6, 14–17).

Scholars debate whether the woman here represents the church or the mother of Jesus. The Catholic tradition identifies her as the mother of Jesus, while not denying the application to the church. The male child, who is God's 'Christ' (Rev. 12.10), is her biological child, not that of the church. The church is his body (Col. 1.18; Eph. 2.23); he gave birth to her by his pierced side on the cross, as the fathers of the church long recognized. In John's Gospel, Mary is designated as both 'woman' and 'the mother of Jesus' (2.1–12; 19.25–27). For Paul, she is the 'woman' from whom God's Son was born at 'the fullness of time' (Gal. 4.4). 'The Lion of the tribe of Judah, the root of David' (Rev. 5.5–6) is equally 'the Son of Mary' (Mark 6.3); he received his Davidic root through her (Matt. 1.6, 16). The church uses Rev. 12.1–17 as the first reading for the feast of Mary's Assumption into heaven. This feast marks her full participation in the redemptive work of Christ, her own God-given final victory over Satan, sin and death.

Secondly, the double flight of the woman and her newborn child (to the desert and to God's throne) evokes Herod's plot to kill Jesus, and the consequent flight into Egypt (Matt. 2.7–8, 13–18); this later became a flight into Galilee (Matt. 2.19–23). When Herod did not succeed in killing the child, he, like the dragon, 'waged war' on innocent children who can be said to have triumphed 'by the blood of the Lamb' and given witness for Jesus by their death (cf. 12.11, 17). The church celebrates them on 28 December as the Holy Innocents and identifies them as the 144,000 who follow the Lamb because they had never lied (Rev. 14.1–5).

After his decisive defeat by the woman and her offspring, Satan turns attention to the rest of the woman's children (Rev. 12.17). In the light of John 19.26, any disciple loved by Jesus becomes his mother's child. Satan's war against the rest of the woman's children is like striking at her offspring's heel. Once 'victory and power and empire for ever have been won by our God and all authority for his Christ', (12.10), the defeat of the devil is assured and is only a matter of time (21.5). This 'victory', without the article, is absolute. The event in 12.1–17 thus looks to Rev. 21–22 for its dénouement.

Revelation 21–22 recaptures the first creation (Gen. 1.1–2.4). Since the first creation was symbolically accursed as a result of Adam's sin (Gen. 3.17; 'soil' here representing creation), the final defeat of Satan through whom this curse came about necessitates the redemption of creation itself; hence the rationale for the creation of the new heaven and the new earth. Noticeably, Satan with his agents, his beast and false prophet (Rev. 20.7–10), and Death and Hades (20.14), are thrown into the lake of sulphur before the appearance of the new heaven and earth, or the establishment of the reign of God and his saints.

This order of events ensures that the new creation will be totally free of the evil influence of Satan and his agents. Since the beast and the false prophet were the principal agents who deceived and won followers for Satan/the dragon (Rev. 13.1–17), they are the first to be thrown into this lake of sulphur (20.19–20). Death, the last enemy (cf. I Cor. 15.26) is destroyed last. Their overthrow is described as 'the second death'. Yet though final victory is established, Satan is not annihilated. Only his inimical power over humanity with that of his agents is destroyed.

The new heaven and earth have no need of sun or moon, since God himself is the light (21.23). The earth/soil, originally created good (Gen. 1.11–12; 2.9), but accursed because of sin, is now so fertile that its trees bear fruit twelve months of the year. The tree of the knowledge of good and evil, whose forbidden fruit brought death, disappears (Gen. 2.16–17); only 'the trees of life' (now plural), with leaves for the healing of the nations, remain (Rev. 22.2). The motifs of light, water and river that accompanied the first creation resurface in this new creation (cf. Gen. 1.3–4, 9–10; 2.10–14; Rev. 21.5; 22.1–2).

Those who in life disobeyed God naturally join Satan and Death in the lake of sulphur (20.15; 21.8). All evildoers are prohibited entrance into the new Jerusalem, the city of God (Rev. 21.27), just as previously fallen Adam and Eve were forbidden entrance into the Garden (Gen. 3.23–24). In the first heaven and earth, God left humanity largely to itself, but with occasional visits (Gen. 3.8). Now God comes much closer to them; he makes his home among them (Rev. 21.3; 22.3–5). God's permanent presence guarantees the permanence of the victory of the redeemed over Satan and his agents.

The motifs common to the first creation accounts (Gen. 1.1–2: 4; 2.5–25) and Rev. 12; 21–22 listed here are not exhaustive. But they lead one to conclude that the author of Revelation consciously drew on the first accounts in communicating his message. The canonists who gave the Bible its final shape may or may not have been aware of the full significance of this canonical shape as discussed here. But its message that evil will eventually be defeated cannot be ignored.

This apocalyptic and essentially biblical faith rests on the solid grounds of the resurrection of Christ. His is the decisive victory over sin and death. His resurrection is foundational to the entire Christian faith (I Cor. 15.3–5, 14, 16–19). The whole message of Revelation itself rests on it (cf. Rev. 1.18–19). John's Gospel speaks of Jesus as 'the resurrection' and the life (11.25–26); the one through whom the dead are raised and judged (5.25–29).

The relevance of apocalyptic for today

The question now needs to be asked, does apocalyptic have any relevance to our post-modern, technological world? Or was it simply a pious wish of ancient people who needed to console themselves with empty hopes in time of suffering, by believing that God would eventually intervene decisively to redress their ills by creating a sin-free world order? Is apocalyptic an escape from the hard realities of life?

As said earlier, apocalyptic is concerned with the evil present in the human heart and systems. There is need to identify the forms which this evil takes in our times. The prostitute (Revelation 17–18) is the antithesis of the woman in 12.1–17; she represents the Roman empire, the superpower of the time, and specializes in intoxicating kings and merchants (18.3), but is eventually destroyed. As C. H. Giblin has pointed out, the condemnation of this evil empire is not restricted to the Roman empire. It applies to all evil, corrupt and oppressive systems of all ages, be they political, economic, technological, social, racial, cultural, religious or moral.[5]

If this is so, then today more than ever the Christian needs to be reminded of the importance of apocalyptic faith. To take one example, 'the Economy', the modern 'god', can be compared to the dragon and its beasts (Rev. 12–13). Like the dragon, it has its beasts and false prophets, to whom it has delegated its powers, this time of the market and free trade. Its promoting agents might be G 7, the IMF, the World Bank, the Paris Club and multi-national corporations. They know how to prevent people from buying or selling unless they worship this modern dragon. Its empire might be 'globalization', a double-faced entity. Deceitfully it promises its clients (be they rich or poor) a happiness which it has no powers to give, but often takes away.

The global economy and the powers of the market devour all but its architects. Nations are valued for their economic viability; their ranking in the world community depends on the strength or weakness of their economy. 'Third World' nations, especially of Africa, who cannot join the club, are simply treated as expendable. At best they serve as a dumping ground for toxic waste, obsolete technology, expired drugs and as a viable market for arms sale. In order to belong, heads of state and top military personnel in Africa have despoiled their peoples' heritage and sacrificed it at its altar. The 'developed' world has benefitted and still benefits from the victuals of this sacrifice. At times the despoiled nations themselves receive crumbs, as aid, from their own economic banquets, that their corrupt and misguided leaders have stolen and given to the 'developed' nations to enjoy.

But, this state of affairs notwithstanding, is it conceivable that the cataclysmic destruction predicted in Revelation will ever happen? One may answer this question by recalling that when God made the first promise in Gen. 3.15 (the proto-evangelium), it took thousands of unrecordable years for that promise to be fulfilled in God's 'fullness of time' (Gal. 4.4). The same applies relatively to the promises made to Abraham, the patriarchs and Israel. Though greatly delayed, these promises were eventually fulfilled by the one who made them (cf. Heb. 11.39–40).

Apocalyptic faith believes in God's absolute sovereignty over creation and sees God as ultimately destroying evil, unjust and oppressive systems of whatever order; it cannot be dismissed as irrelevant for our post-modern technological world. Humanity tends to become more and more self-sufficient because of its technological achievements. But discovering the riches of creation and putting them generally to selfish use are no guarantee that such exploitative systems will not eventually crumble. Apocalyptic faith is connected with the Parousia (cf. Mark 13.26); it looks for its fulfilment to the same God who made and fulfilled the previous promises. That it will happen is certain; but how and when, are known only to God (cf. Mark 13.32–33 and parallels).

In conclusion, this study sought to demonstrate that apocalyptic faith is made necessary by the biblical doctrine of creation and the fall. Its primary concern is the final eradication of evil and the restoration of the good in creation according to God's original design. This apocalyptic faith is essentially a biblical faith; it finds its solid base in Christ's resurrection. The reader is invited to reflect on this faith and identify and courageously face the challenges which it poses in his or her local and global contexts.

Notes

1. H. de Baar, *The Bible on the Final Coming*, De Pere, Wisconsin 1965, 57–64, gives a succinct historical survey of such efforts.

2. Brevard Childs, *Introduction to the Old Testament as Scripture*, London and Philadelphia 1979.

3. This is true both of works that are totally apocalyptic in genre (e.g., the extra-canonical apocalypses of Isaiah and I Enoch, the canonical books of Revelation and Daniel) and of apocalyptic sections of such works as Zech. 1.7–6.15; Ezekiel 37; 40–44; and Mark 13 and parallels.

4. On the apocalyptic character of the Bible, cf. R. R. Wilson, 'From Prophecy to Apocalyptic: Reflections on the Shape of Israelite Religion', *Semeia* 21, 1982, 79–95; J. C. Beker, *Paul's Apocalyptic Gospel: The Coming Triumph of God*, Philadelphia 1982; John J. Collins, 'The Apocalyptic Context of Christian Origins: The Bible and Its Traditions', *Michigan Quarterly Review* 22/2, 1983, 250–64.

5. C. H. Giblin, *The Book of Revelation: The Open Book of Prophecy*, Good News Studies 34, Collegeville, Minnesota 1991, 166.

Reading The Book of Revelation Today

Respecting its Originality while Recognizing its Lasting Message

Håkan Ulfgard

As the year 2000 is rapidly drawing near, it may often be noted how secular fascination with the approaching date is taking on a semi-religious dimension coloured by eschatological ideas about the end of the world. Still, it should be remembered that for the world's large non-Christian majority there can be no possible religious significance at all attached to the turn of the millennia in our standardized, universal time-reckoning.[1] But among various Christian denominations around the world the feeling of living in the last days of world history is being promoted by church leaders, preachers and writers. Claiming to possess true knowledge about God's secret plans for the world, the practical consequences of their authoritative interpretations include such extremes as stockpiling food for consumption during the cataclysmic years to come, and even voluntary suicide in the conviction of being the first to enjoy the awaited salvation. Less drastically, other followers of their call for alertness join in intensified prayer, Bible study and mental preparation for the new age.

However, this obsession with God's plans for the future of the world, and with finding the signs of the end in the contemporary situation, is not a new phenomenon among Christians. There is a biblical heritage of strong interest in things to come, good or bad; and from time to time in the history of Christianity, often related to periods of crisis – real or perceived –, there has been a notable increase in eschatological speculation. In his fascinating study *When Time Shall Be No More*.

Prophecy Belief in Modern American Culture,[2]   P. Boyer has brought
together an immense documentation on the fascination for speculation
about the end among Christians of the last two centuries. Richly
documented with quotations from people like John Nelson Darby, Cyrus
Scofield, Billy Graham, Hal Lindsey, Pat Robertson and many more, his
book gives abundant evidence of the obsession in important parts of the
modern Northern American cultural milieu with the literal fulfilment of
the biblical prophecies, as if they had been specifically written with the
nineteenth or twentieth centuries in mind.[3]

Though described mainly as an American phenomenon, limited to
various evangelical denominations, this expression of modern Christianity is part of a larger process. As Boyer rightly observes, it is a result of
the 'democratic' and 'rationalistic' ideal of Bible reading which became
widespread from the last century onwards. People were encouraged to
read the Bible for themselves, always trying to find a personal application
of its content. With this attitude followed the assumption that even its
symbolic data, such as its chronological figures, could be translated into
concrete conditions and applied to the present situation. In shaping a
popular Christian mentality, the particular form of American belief in
prophecy has had far-reaching consequences for the actualization of the
eschatological concepts of the Bible. By relating present events and
conditions to biblical statements about God's awaited salvation and
judgment, it has been very influential in creating an atmosphere of
heightened alert, also fuelled by global ideological, political and military
tensions: 'Be Prepared – The End Is Near! The Time Is Now!' However,
the success of the various actualizing interpretations seems to depend
more on their ability to meet the expectations and demands of their
audience than on their congruence with the historically-conditioned
message of the biblical texts themselves.

The disputed book of Revelation

With its visionary imagery, chronological calculation, and expectation of
God's final vindication of the righteous and judgment of his enemies, the
Revelation to John in particular has come into focus as the Christian
source-book and timetable for finding the signs of the end in the present
(though other biblical texts have been influential as well, especially the
Book of Daniel). At the same time, it is one of the biblical books that
offers the greatest difficulties for its interpreters, and it has also often
been regarded as the least 'Christian' book of the New Testament –
remember Rudolf Bultmann's verdict on it as 'weakly Christianized

Judaism'.[4] 'Unlike the four Gospels, the book of Acts, and the letters of the New Testament, one looks in vain here for concrete information about the earthly Jesus and the early church. Also, there is nothing of the Pauline theological reasoning and its parænetic consequences. On the contrary, a certain anti-Pauline attitude may be detected in its harsh ethics and total rejection of the Roman state. Instead, what we find is a prophetic message about the imminent end of the world, wrapped in an epistolary framework, and expressed in series of dramatic visions whose symbolic language and grotesque imagery have throughout the history of its interpretation fascinated, terrified and dismayed its readers. No wonder that Revelation has often been the focus of intense polemic, mostly concerning the realization of its prophecies in relation to other Christian concepts about the future, and that it has often been considered as of no value for Christian teaching or preaching.

Disused and abused – how do we read Revelation today? Is there anything in its prophetic message that still speaks to us, regardless of whether we consider ourselves as living in the final days or not? Or should it be rejected entirely as a bizarre remnant of the first Christian generation's obsession with speculation about the imminent return of Christ and the end of the world, or as the product of a sick mind? Should the sad – and mad – story of its actualization in various premillennarian dispensationalist schemes in recent centuries, especially in the USA, render it useless among Christians less willing to heed the calls of born-again charismatic figures and calculating commercialized vendors on the Christian market?

The answer is 'Yes' and 'No'. Revelation certainly has a lasting message for Christians today. There is no reason to reject it altogether because of the speculative interpretation from which it has suffered. But it should be respected for what it is, and purports to be: a prophetic message carrying a unique witness of early Christian belief – less interested, it must be admitted, in speaking about the earthly Jesus and his followers (as in the Gospels and Acts), or in sketching the contours of a Christian life in the multicultural Greco-Roman world (as in the rest of the New Testament), than in focussing on questions about the consequences of Christ's resurrection for the world in general and for his faithful in particular. What really ought to be put in question is the kind of hermeneutic that has so long produced fanciful and distorting images under the guise of pious or charismatic interpretation – and for this, Boyer's book is excellent reading.

A hopeful sign is the shift in recent years among scholars towards appreciating the qualities of Revelation as a literary and dramatic whole.

To borrow a formulation from the title of a pioneering study in this vein by Adela Yarbro Collins, the 'power of the Apocalypse' to invoke the imaginative participation of its readers or listeners (cf. 1.3) in the drama contained its visions has been more and more acknowledged.[5] This changing attitude is clearly to be detected in the later studies on Revelation by Elizabeth Schüssler Fiorenza, in which she pays special attention to how the symbolic universe created through its mythopoeic language functions to comfort and exhort its readers/listeners, challenging them to identify their own self-understanding and experience as Christians with its story.[6] A similar perspective also permeates the more recent, important study by Leonard L. Thompson, *The Book of Revelation: Apocalypse and Empire*.[7] While playing down the idea of an acute crisis as the historical background for the writing of Revelation, he regards it as a literary product which attempts to transfer into a holistic vision a certain perception of early Christian life in a Hellenistic surrounding, thus presenting a story with which its readers can identify.

Approaching the book of Revelation as literature

The difficult task of reading Revelation in quest of its possible message to modern readers while at the same time respecting its original context calls for an awareness of the pitfalls of both a too narrowly historical approach and an uncritical juxtaposition of past and present conditions. However, its rhetorical possibilities may be drawn upon for present-day application, without thereby neglecting the roots of its symbolic language.

One fundamental prerequisite is that the literary-dramatic qualities of Revelation should be fully acknowledged. While Martin Karrer has rightly stressed the epistolary aspects of John's visionary message,[8] Adela Yarbro Collins (cf. above) has pointed to the cathartic function of his dramatic story as the reader is taken through the series of earthly catastrophes and heavenly worship until the final return of the conditions of paradise. Despite the highly Jewish character of Revelation (to which I return below), the author's indebtedness to imagery from the Greco-Roman cultural context should not be overlooked, as has been amply illustrated by e.g. David E. Aune and Colin Hemer.[9] Roman imperial court imagery and local conditions in the seven cities to which Revelation is directed may be reflected in its heavenly scenery and in the 'letters' to the churches in chs. 2–3.

But what I would like to draw special attention to is the simple fact that the story of Revelation contains all the elements listed by Aristotle in his *Ars Poetica* as essential components in dramatic literature, particularly in the tragedies, but also in epic texts: plot, character, diction, thought, spectacle, and song (cf. 6.9).[10] In view of the obvious scenic character of Revelation with all its visionary imagery, dramatic episodes and choirs of heavenly voices commenting on events in heaven and on earth, commentators have shown remarkably little interest in this particular aspect of its literary quality.[11] It is especially interesting to note that there is no comparable dramatic 'story' in the roughly contemporary Jewish apocalypses IV Ezra and II Baruch. Even if it cannot be proved that the author of Revelation was consciously following the Aristotelian ideal, it is striking that there are many more scenic qualities in his text as compared to what one finds in these Jewish apocalypses. In a masterly manner, traditional Jewish apocalyptic imagery is adapted into a literary fabric which still creates a powerful reading experience when treated as a whole, continuous drama – perhaps even more in our era of visualized communication. The dialectic between scenes of heavenly worship and earthly catastrophes, with voices in heaven proclaiming God's victory and commenting on its effects on earth, provides a scenic setting for the drama unfolding in the successive series of seven seals, trumpets and bowls, with their revealing interludes (e.g. in chs. 7 and 12–14). Rather than trying to 'explain' every single image and trying to match it with contemporary events at the time of the author, one should read John's story as a whole, a continuous narrative with internal allusions, dramatic highpoints, and anticipations of its ending.

If this may be taken as a sign of Hellenistic influence on John's writing, a way of seeking an effective means to communicate his message to his audience, which still functions to fascinate modern readers, his fundamental conceptual world is thoroughly Jewish. To respect this fact is a *sine qua non* if one wants to understand the basic thrust of his book and to appreciate its relevance for modern Christians. The recognition of this Jewish character does not at all mean that its Christian significance is diminished (against Bultmann, see above). On the contrary, it serves as a necessary reminder of the concrete and spiritual roots of the church, and, what is even more important, it gives some crucial clues for understanding the lasting message and relevance of the Book of Revelation.

Approaching the Book of Revelation within its Jewish Christian context

First of all it is necessary to be aware that John's preoccupation with the end is quite understandable in view of early Jewish Christian belief. Jesus appeared as the Messiah when the time was fulfilled, and was expected to return imminently in glory. The beginning of confrontation with the Roman authorities and with non-believing Jews was regarded as a sign of the fore-ordained suffering, *thlipsis*, of the end-time. But the idea of living close to the end did not originate among Christians. As shown especially by the Qumran texts, the idea of living in the final days (*acharit ha-yamim*) had already for a long time been a fundamental concept in a 'reform' group who considered themselves as the 'New Covenant' (cf. CD 6.19; 19.33; 20.12). Using chronological data in the biblical prophecies in Jeremiah, Ezekiel and Daniel, they took a great interest in calculating God's future intervention on behalf of his chosen righteous.

In both cases, however, the Qumranite and Christian self-understanding of being the holy community of the end-time resulted in a transcendence of chronological and spatial categories: through membership of the community of the elect, and by the grace of God, the faithful on earth could be considered as united with the company of worshipping angels around God's throne in heaven, celebrating and even sharing his absolute royal dominion, his *basileia*. In Qumran, this human sharing in the realities of the heavenly world was assured by the observation of the strictest rules of priestly purity.

In Revelation, which addresses Jews as well as non-Jews, the introductory greeting in 1.5–6 functions as a decisive clue for shaping a common identity and self-understanding as members of the people of the Lamb. After stating that Jesus loves them (present tense!) and has liberated them from their sins, the author goes on to proclaim that they have been made 'a kingdom, priests serving his [the Lamb's] God and Father'. By identifying his readers with the covenantal people of Israel in the biblical Exodus story (cf. Exod. 19.6), the author not only opens the way for further allusions to the Exodus in his visionary story – clearly to be seen e.g. in the series of trumpets and bowls (chs. 8–9; 16) and in the 'song of Moses' by the sea (ch. 15). He also emphasizes their new dignity as being admitted to the closest possible relationship with God and with the heavenly world, a traditional royal and priestly privilege. His universal scope emerges clearly from the repeated phrase 'every tribe and language and people and nation' (5.9; cf. 7.9; 10.11; 11.9; 13.7; 14.6; 17.15).[12]

But it is typical of the particular use of scripture in Revelation – which has a great deal in common with what one finds in the Qumran literature – that biblical allusions have multiple meanings. The image of God's chosen people as a holy priesthood in the coming era of salvation is also found in Isa. 61.6. The readers are therefore invited to identify themselves both with the conventional people of Israel, proclaimed as 'a priestly kingdom and a holy nation' in Exod. 19.6, and with Isaiah's purified priesthood that will serve God in the restored and glorified Jerusalem. This explains how God's chosen people in the dramatic visionary imagery of John's writing can be envisaged both *before* the expected final tribulation, being on their way to the Promised Land, and *after* passing through this ordeal, enjoying heavenly blessing in the presence of God (see the enumeration of the 144,000 from Israel's twelve tribes in 7.1–8, followed by the vision of the great multitude from all nations, tribes, peoples and languages in 7.9–17).[13] Thus, having pursued his visionary story through the repeated scenes of judgment and salvation, in his final vision of a new heaven and earth, of the New Jerusalem, and of paradise regained (21.1–22.5), John reverts to the priestly dignity of the chosen and saved. His depiction of the future realization of the kingdom of God in the new world, where no evil powers can harm his creation, ends with God's ransomed priestly people in total communion with God. It should especially be noted how the Isaianic prophecies about the future glory of Zion (chs. 60–62) are applied to the ideal community of believers.

Another phrase which functions as a key text for understanding the Christian self-understanding of Revelation is found in 1.9. Even more than the idea of the ransomed community of believers as a 'royal priesthood', it also holds a powerful rhetorical potential for the present. After saluting his addressees, John begins the account of his visionary drama by telling them that he shares with them 'in Jesus the persecution and the kingdom and the patient endurance'. These words summarize the particular eschatological perspective of the whole book: Christian existence is a paradoxical juxtaposition of earthly trial and heavenly bliss while waiting for final consummation – all these qualifications held together by being 'in Christ'. The full meaning of this introductory statement has unfortunately all too often been distorted particularly by being deferred to the distant future. But in reality, John is speaking about the present situation of himself and of his readers as they have been incorporated into the Christ-event, liberated from their sins through the blood of Jesus. Their existence has taken on a new dimension, especially the awareness of living in the era of scriptural fulfilment and in the final days of the world. The paradoxical outcome of this eschatological consciousness is that the believers can be regarded as sharing at the same time both the awaited suffering of the end-time and the royal dominion envisaged for the future.[14]

Transcendence and transformation: understanding the lasting message of the book of Revelation

To conclude these brief observations on how to approach the Book of Revelation today, respecting its originality while recognizing its lasting message, maybe the anthropological concepts of *'communitas'* and 'liminality' could be useful.[15] Through the use of apocalyptic imagery and a wealth of scriptural allusions, the prophet John wishes to confirm to his readers/listeners their experience of having been set apart from the rest of the world. As members of the eschatological people of the Lamb they are exhorted and encouraged to adapt their lives to the transcendent reality of God's universal rule, soon to be realized fully at the return of Jesus. Far more than presenting a timetable for the future, the drama of Revelation speaks in a mystic fashion about the challenge and comfort of living in two worlds at the same time.

Notes

1. The fact is that we are already past the 2000-year milestone if Jesus was born under the rule of Herod the Great, who died in 4 BC (the dating of his birth in Matt. 2.1 is commonly preferred to that in Luke 2.2).

2. Cambridge, Mass. and London 1992.

3. See B. McGinn, *Antichrist. Two Thousand Years of the Human Fascination with Evil*, San Francisco 1994, 252–62.

4. R. Bultmann, *The Theology of the New Testament*, London and New York 1955, Vol. 2, 175.

5. See A. Yarbro Collins, *Crisis and Catharsis: The Power of the Apocalypse*, Philadelphia 1984.

6. See E. Schüssler Fiorenza, *The Book of Revelation – Justice and Judgment*, Philadelphia 1985.

7. New York and Oxford 1990.

8. M. Karrer, *Die Johannesoffenbarung als Brief. Studien zu ihrem literarischen, historischen und theologischen Ort*, FRLANT 140, Göttingen 1986.

9. D. E. Aune, 'The Influence of Roman Imperial Court Ceremonial on the Apocalypse of John', *Biblical Research* 28, 1983, 5–26; C. J. Hemer, *The Letters to the Seven Churches of Asia in Their Local Settings*, JSNT Suppl 11, Sheffield 1986.

10. Aristotle, *The Poetics*, Loeb Classical Library, London and Cambridge, Mass. 1960.

11. Among the few studies of this kind, see J. Bowman, *The Drama of the Book of Revelation*, Philadelphia 1955: the later study by J. L. Blevins, *Revelation as Drama*, Nashville 1984, is less relevant.

12. Note the repeated insistence on the royal priesthood of God's chosen people in 5.10.

13. See also 15.2–4.

14. Precisely this juxtaposition of an experience of the tribulation of the end-time and of the idea of sharing royal dignity and dominion is witnessed in many cases by the Qumran texts, see e.g. A. M. Schwemer, 'Gott als König und seine Königs-herrschaft in den Sabbatliedern aus Qumran', in *Königsherrschaft Gottes und himmlischer Kult im Judentum. Urchristentum und in der hellenistisehen Welt*, ed. M. Hengel and A. M. Schwemer, Tübingen 1991, 45–118.

15. See the studies by V. Turner et al., *The Ritual Process: Structure and Anti-Structure*. Chicago 1969, but see also J. -P. Ruiz, 'Betwixt and Between on the Lord's Day: Liturgy and the Apocalypse', *Society of Biblical Literature 1992 Seminar Papers*, ed. E. H. Lovering, Atlanta, Ga. 1992, 654–72.

Imagining the End: The Augustinian Dynamics of Expectation

Lewis Ayres

I. Introduction

The last few years have seen a great deal of literature on the subject of 'millenarianism' and 'apocalypticism'. In this literature the apocalyptic or millenarian (the terms are often used very widely) strand in Christian tradition is often described as the result of Christianity's initial expectation of an imminent end being postponed indefinitely. This postponement was never quite able to overcome the sense of imminent end implanted in those first momentous years, and thus apocalyptic movements could easily flourish under the right pressures, often attaching themselves to all manner of perceived 'ends' indicated by various calendars and dating systems.

At the same time as offering this interpretation, much of this recent literature uses the theme in Christian tradition as a point of departure for considering a much wider range of cultural phenomena, and indeed we might identify two constants of this literature: the attempt to find such an explanation at the level of social or economic law; and insistence on a strong division between the terms 'eschatology' and 'apocalyptic' – the former being the reasonable, tame, sometimes institutionally acceptable, face of the latter.[1] Although it is difficult to generalize here, apocalyptic is often described as marked by supposedly reliable prediction of the imminent and identifiable end of things (or of the events which are the commencement of that end), while eschatology is supposedly marked by claims that one cannot know the 'day or the hour', and the use of eschatological passages from the scriptures as allegorical of contemporary life. The distinction is often emphasized by identifying proponents of the two sides as belonging to different social categories, or by placing great emphasis on the claim to predict when the events of the end will take place. This last division has been particularly clear in discussion of early and mediaeval Christian thought.

I suggest that in this rush to identify general cultural categories, a number of mistakes have been made concerning these attitudes in their Christian form, and that theologians themselves might here be seduced into ignoring a fundamental and *necessary* theological continuum between such movements and mainstream Christianity. In this article I will take just one example, though an example often taken to be pivotal: Augustine of Hippo (AD 354–430). I hope to show how Augustine's thought demonstrates the continuum between such claims and the character of the eschatological imagination that all Christians *should* possess. Thus, by challenging some recent interpretations of this one example, lines of questioning may be indicated for many other cases. My alternative presentation will depend on identifying 'eschatology' and 'apocalyptic' as *different* points along a *continuum* of scriptural inter-pretation.

II. The dynamics of Augustine's eschatology

Augustine has often been presented as the archetypal 'spiritualizing', 'Platonizing' interpreter of eschatology. In AD 410 Rome itself was sacked by Alaric's Goths, an event which caused fear throughout the Roman world.[2] The fear followed not so much from the actual economic or strategic importance of Rome at that time as from the symbolic place of Rome in the culture of the Roman world. For many this event seemed to signal the approaching judgment and the end of all things, despite the fact that no contemporary dating systems presented the year as one of great significance. Augustine's response was, in his great work *De civitate Dei*, to emphasize that predicting the actual date of the end was not within human capabilities. One recent author goes so far as to describe this view as 'the sensible Augustinian view', which should be seen as arguing against those groups and movements who saw the end as not only imminent but predictable.[3]

Stephen O'Leary's *Arguing the Apocalypse* presents Augustine as pivotal point in the development of early and mediaeval Christian 'eschatology' and 'apocalyptic', arguing that he both postpones indefi-nitely the event of the end and concomitantly enables a certain dualism to infect Christian accounts of existence: the division between good and evil now occurs not only at the end but in each Christian life.[4] O'Leary's interpretation makes use of Kenneth Burke's terms 'tragic' and 'comic', which may need some clarification. The 'tragic' concerns characters and plots which move towards 'unhappy' endings, and conceives of evil as guilt to be answered by inevitable punishment, while the 'comic' plot builds towards a happy ending and ends with the exposing of fallibility. The tragic sees the progress of things as essentially unchangeable, while the comic admits of change and the chance of redemption (thus they should not be taken as two degrees of seriousness). O'Leary writes,

> in Augustine's comic reading, the ultimate features of the divine plan remain inscrutable to believers and non-believers alike . . . In the tragic periodization of history, calamities appear as part of a pre-determined sequence that will culminate in the reign of Antichrist, whose final defeat will be followed by the millennial kingdom. In Augustine's provisionally comic view of history, calamities become episodes, recurrent events that all human communities must face without recourse to an apocalyptic understanding, while the millennial kingdom becomes an allegory of the present age . . . The comic interpretation of the Apocalypse thus neutralizes its predictive function.[5]

In O'Leary's terminology a 'predictive' interpretation of John's Apocalypse emphasizes the inevitability of the end and provides a resource for reading the present age as a series of signs pointing to that end. An 'anti-predictive' use, such as Augustine is supposed to illustrate, emphasizes a 'comic' strand of the story in which the story provides resources for analysing current fallibility and outlining possibilities for change. However, note that O'Leary's analysis links together being able to predict the time of the end with being able to predict its details and temporal structure. He claims Augustine as *non*-predictive because of Augustine's unwillingness to see individual events as firm and reliable predictions of the time of the end. After offering his account he adds that, of course, Augustine still hangs on to the traditional description of Christ's coming in judgment: but this, for O'Leary, only functions to add a 'comic' dimension to the drama. I will argue that this admission reveals the unsatisfactory nature of O'Leary's analysis: while Augustine clearly does resist the tendency of some contemporaries to see contemporary events as signs of the end that deliver certain knowledge of its timing, he *does* constantly emphasize both the importance of our faith in the structure of the end and the importance of our viewing present events within our sense of the approaching end of things.

In order to see how this might be so, we need to see how Augustine's concerns for appropriately formed faith and for coherent biblical interpretation shape his treatment of eschatology.[6] In particular Augustine exhibits a dynamic between attention to the details of the sources for Christian eschatology (such passages as Daniel 12; Revelation; I Cor. 1.15; John 14–18; and some Gospel material) and the need to keep the overall 'shape' of one's faith consistently focussed and formed. We can begin by noting some aspects of the argument in Book 20 of Augustine's *De civitate Dei*.[7]

Augustine's discussion in the first half of Book 20 (which overall is concerned to set out an interpretation of the events at the *eschaton*), both emphasizes that God judges (often inscrutably) even now (*Civ.* 20, 2), and clearly sets out to discuss what will happen at that time when the final judgment occurs. Augustine's drawing out of 'evidence' for his account of these events is specifically aimed at those who, paralleling Christ's opponents in Matthew 11.22, doubt the significance of the works through which God's power has been demonstrated (*Civ.* 20, 5ff.). Throughout the book it is essential that a firm and 'predictable' basic sequence of events may be trustworthily discerned from scripture, and that we grasp the importance of that sequence even amid the complex differing interpretations of this scriptural material.

At *Civ.* 20, 7 Augustine turns to a discussion of Rev. 20.1–6, the passage in which the notion of the first resurrection and the thousand-year reign of the saints becomes clear:

> 20.1 Then I saw an angel coming down from heaven . . . ²And he seized . . . the Devil . . . and bound him for a thousand years, ³and threw him into the pit, and shut it and sealed it over him . . . till the thousand years were ended. After that he must be loosed for a little while. ⁴. . . Also I saw the souls of those who had been beheaded for their testimony to Jesus . . . They came to life and reigned with Christ a thousand years. ⁵The rest of the dead did not come to life until the thousand years were ended. This is the first resurrection.

Augustine states that at an earlier stage he had interpreted this passage as indicating a literal thousand-year period after the end of the sixth age of the world and thought of the saints as then experiencing a spiritual foretaste of their life after the judgment. However, he has now changed his mind, and harbours a suspicion that the majority of those who think of this thousand years in a literal, material way also conceive of the saints then experiencing *material* delight (unlike his own earlier interpretation), a possibility that seems to fit ill with the importance of controlling our material desires if we are to attain heaven. Augustine (precisely and usefully) terms those who believe materially in both aspects Chiliasts or Millenarians. He does not refute these opinions in detail, but instead offers his own account of the key six verses.

Interestingly he begins by allowing the possibility of *two* interpretations of this thousand years: it may either be an actual period in the last, the sixth, age of the world (through which we are now passing[8]) *or* it may be intended to stand for the whole. He has ruled out, for reasons not discussed, his own earlier idea that this was a seventh age, but still allows for those who take the thousand years as a literal period. However, for Augustine, it is more persuasive to take the 'perfection' of the number 1,000 as indicating that it is to be read as indicating *all* of the period between Christ's first coming and the period in which the devil is loosed for a final attack on the City of God, the kingdom of heaven, that is, the church. Concerning this 'loosing' of the devil Augustine remains firmly literal, envisaging (following Daniel) a period of three and a half actual years. During the 'thousand' years Christ rules through his 'body', the church, and even during the period when the devil is 'free', God's power will ensure that the church stands firm.

For Augustine the choice one makes about the thousand years is in part dependent on the particular trope one takes to be in operation in this text, Augustine preferring the second of the options he offers. However, it is also important to notice Augustine's concern to present an account that will be consonant with his other accounts of the character of Christian existence and especially with his emphasis elsewhere on the priority of God's action in redemption. Thus, to take one example, it is essential for us to understand the sequence of events at the end in such a way that we do not overturn the priority and dependability of God's action which forms such an essential part of how we understand Christian existence now. Thinking of the devil gaining the ability to draw Christians away from the church during this final short period is possible only as long as we understand that those who are drawn away are drawn into their predestined fate (*Civ.* 20, 11–12). To take one more example, the character of the rule of the saints during this 'thousand-year' period, whether understood literally or not, must conform to our account of how the saints will reign in Christ when the goal of the final 'Sabbath' is reached (*Civ.* 20, 9).

In these examples one can see a deep concern for the mutual interaction between our interpretation of the *eschaton* and our interpretation of this life now. I suggest that this is best understood by seeing how, for Augustine, one's reading of scripture must result in beliefs consistent with and formative of the form of life that one thinks central to Christian existence.

III. Augustine and the dynamics of scriptural interpretation

Two inter-related dynamics are at work in Augustine's interpretation of the texts discussed in the previous section. One concerns Augustine's understanding of the function of faith and hope within the drama of redemption, while the second concerns the nature of scriptural interpretation, and functions within the context of the first dynamic. I will discuss these dynamics in order.

Elsewhere I have tried to show that there is a christological context for the *exercitatio* of body and soul which, for Augustine, we all need to undergo.[9] All Christian existence in this stage of the redemptive 'drama' – between Ascension and Judgment – is characterized by Christ's presence as Word, and yet his absence in his human nature. This structure of presence and absence is intended to highlight and meet the need for our human natures and imaginations to be reformed so that we may learn to 'see' the Word's presence in all things. Such a reformation, which comes through an inseparable combination of the practice of charity and through formation in attention to the scriptures (in a variety of settings, including the liturgical[10]), will enable us to become ready for the completion of the union between the 'body' of Christ and its 'head' in the beatific vision. In the *City of God* Augustine speaks of this union thus: 'ultimately those people reign with him who are in [Christ's] kingdom in such a way that they themselves *are* his kingdom' (*Civ.* 20, 9) – a statement which, as becomes apparent a little later in the work, needs to be understood within his theology of the body of Christ (e.g. *Civ.* 22, 18; 29–30).

Within this stage of the redemptive drama the relationship between faith and hope is vital. Both faith and hope are of things unseen, but for Augustine, hope in its theological sense concerns 'only . . . things that are good *and* which lie only in the future *and* which have a relevance to him who is said to entertain it'.[11] Appropriate faith provides the basis for our reasonable hope: we have faith in many categories of things, good and evil things, but the structure and interaction between the objects of our faith enable a hope to emerge which will in turn provide a direction for our lives. 'Appropriate' in the previous sentence is a complex term corresponding to Latin rhetorical terms such as *convenientia* and *aptum*, which were used by Augustine to indicate the way that God's action towards us in Christ is 'rhetorically' shaped for and appropriate to our particular needs, with the result that we will respond to and be drawn towards God.[12] Here I am also indicating the importance of belief and action (with which we, through grace, respond to God's 'drawing') being appropriate to the nature of our sinfulness and the nature of the redemptive action into which we are incorporated.

Both faith and hope, as Augustine explains them here, exist always and necessarily in the context of love. Love is symbiotic with and inseparable from hope: love enables hope to take active form and continually demonstrates the immediate consequences of future hope for the construction of present existence.[13] Growth in true love of God, and of things in God, will contribute towards appropriately formed and ordered faith, and that faith will concomitantly facilitate love and hope. This tight relationship motivates and is illustrated by Augustine's hostility towards the 'Academic' philosophical tradition, and towards Cicero when the latter admits doubts about the possibility of an afterlife. In De Trinitate Book XIV Augustine offers an extended critique of Cicero (in other circumstances one of his great sources) which culminates in an attack on the impossibility of forming hope, and thus love, and thus an appropriate form of life, if one ultimately doubts that the final object of one's hope is 'real' (Trin. XIV, 19, 25–26).

It is within this concern for the shaping of faith and hope that one needs to understand the dynamics of Augustine's scriptural interpretation. In his De doctrina Christiana[14] Augustine describes all of scripture as 'nourishing and building up charity and overcoming and conquering vice' (Doc. III, 10, 15), a statement which provides a focus for his discussion of ambiguous passages. He demands continual attention[15] to the structure of the text, and especially attention to those passages whose literal sense clearly indicates something which pertains either to our faith or to our ethical behaviour (and these passages should then be read in a way that renders them consonant with each other). However, within this attention he can also accept a plurality of readings of ambiguous texts as long as they contribute towards the overall end and form of faith, hope and charity for which scripture is providentially ordered.

It should also be noted that texts may have both literal and figurative senses because God enables the events of history to have multiple referral. Thus, it is God's providential ordering of things through creation and continued governance that makes possible figurative reading, and to discern such meanings in things is to discern God's ordered presence. This link between discerning the order of God's redemptive dispensation in scripture and discerning God's presence in things is a theme which may be read in different forms in Augustine's early *De musica* (esp. Book VI) and in the *Confessions*. Most importantly for our purposes, this link indicates that the interaction between reading scripture and 'reading' or 'figuring' the world is the primary site for theological reflection, and that giving an account of the world consonant with the plot and characterization of scripture is a goal towards which we must all strive. Thus, and linking the two main sections of this paper, I suggest that the character of our reading and the way that reading contributes towards the formation of Christian lives (especially the certainties that we allow ourselves and forbid ourselves) is the primary forum in which the debate over the interpretation of John's Apocalypse occurs.

IV. Conclusion

In this article I have considered only one example, although that example is often taken to be pivotal. I have tried to show that Augustine's account of 'eschatology' cannot be very usefully or subtly investigated by placing him within an eschatology/apocalyptic axis. Similarly – and I have not had space to explore this theme here – although there are of course differences between Augustine's interpretations and those of his contemporaries and forebears, these are multiple differences between different readings and interpretations, sometimes overlapping, sometimes not. Indeed, to talk of a possible difference between Augustine and 'his forebears' is already to introduce a false division between the one and the others that is not borne out in Augustine's texts.[16] Lastly, there is, on the basis of this examination, no warrant for describing Augustine as typical of a 'spiritualizing' account of the end. Of course, this discussion of just one point in the story does not provide sufficient proof for that whole account to be reconsidered, but it should unsettle those who wish to hold to that account.

I suggest that discussion of the variety of positions found in discussion of the *eschaton* in early and mediaeval Christian tradition should be seen as a variety of interpretations on a continuum of scriptural interpretation. My approach here is, I hope, compatible with some other recent work on Jewish 'apocalyptic' which strongly questions whether social categories will serve as an adequate heuristic device for exploring different categories of thinking about the end.[17] This is of course not at all to deny that in some cases social force may well stimulate particular forms of exegesis and particular eschatological positions, but rather to indicate that without a more sophisticated set of analytical tools we may miss grasping the deeper assumptions on which all early mediaeval Christian eschatology is based.

Lastly, I would like to draw attention to the importance of the fact that debates over the nature and function of scriptural interpretation are also debates about the relationship between scriptural reading and the possibility of Christian reading and discernment of the world in which we find ourselves. It follows from this that, as may have become clear in the previous section of the article, to understand these debates we will need to become much more sensitive to the intersection of ontological discussion and scriptural interpretation as one of the primary sites for the work of theology. Debates about scriptural interpretation within early Christianity are thus also debates in the area of theology of creation. Indeed, the possibility of our reading these debates clearly may well depend on our ability to understand the differences between pre-modern and modern exegetical concerns, and to see these different (but sometimes overlapping) collections of styles not in terms of progression from one to the other (from pre- to post-critical) but perhaps as competing and as offering different possibilities within the wider development of the relationship between theological exegesis and ontology. Thus, I suggest that the relationship between one's view of scripture and one's view of God's ordering of the world may prove to be the fundamental area of discussion here, and the point at which the dialogue between modern and pre-modern eschatology must be most intense.

Notes

1. Particularly popular in this regard has been N. Cohn, *The Pursuit of the Millenium*, London 1993; see also the variety of accounts in M. Bull (ed.), *Apocalypse Theory and the Ends of the World*, Oxford and Cambridge, MA 1995.

2. See P. Brown, *Augustine of Hippo: A Biography*, London 1977, ch. 25.

3. D. Thompson, *The End of Time: Faith and Fear in the Shadow of the Millenium*, London 1997, 32.

4. S. D. O'Leary, *Arguing the Apocalypse: A Theory of Millennial Rhetoric*, Oxford 1994, 73ff.

5. O'Leary, *Arguing the Apocalypse* (n. 4), 75. A useful recent discussion of comedy and tragedy within the Gospels is to be found in G. Loughlin, *Telling God's Story*, Cambridge 1996, 161ff.

6. Space here does not permit the citation of much primary or secondary literature so for both I indicate B. Daley, *The Hope of the Early Church: A Handbook of Patristic Eschatology*, Cambridge 1991, 131–50 (his discussion of Augustine himself), 281–3 (a selected bibliography).

7. Abbreviations for Augustine's works are from C. P. Mayer (ed.), *Augustinus Lexicon*, Stuttgart and Basel 1986. Quotations from *Civ.* are taken from St. Augustine, *City of God*, tr. J. Bettenson, Harmondsworth 1984. A translation of *Sermon* 259 may be found in J. Rotelle (ed.), *The Works of Saint Augustine, Vol. III/ 7, Sermons (230–272B)*, tr. E. Hill, New York 1993, 177–184. For earlier important considerations of eschatology see *Serm.* 259 (c. AD 400) and *Letter* 199 (c. AD 412).

8. His understanding of the scheme is particularly clear at *Serm.* 259, 2. The first age extends from Adam to Noah, the second from Noah to Abraham, the third from Abraham to David, the fourth from David to the exile, the fifth from the exile to Christ, the sixth from Christ onwards.

9. 'Christology and Faith in Augustine's *De trinitate* XIII: Toward Relocating Books VIII–XV', *Augustinian Studies* 29/1, 1998. The 'drama' referred to here operates entirely in christological terms, but in the light of the previous section one should note that his presentation of the 'six ages' only serves to complement his overall theological structure.

10. See, for example, Augustine's *Letter* 55.

11. *Ench.* 2, 7–8, translated in St Augustine, *Faith, Hope and Charity*, tr. L. A. Arand, Ancient Christian Writers 3, New York 1947, 14–17 (c. AD 420).

12. See H. Lausberg, *Handbuch der Literarischen Rhetorik*, 2 vols., Munich ²1973, §1055–62; §1074–77. For a brief statement of the theory see Cicero, *Or.* 21, 70–71. The link between this aspect of rhetorical theory and the functioning of scripture can also be seen clearly at *Doc.* I, 35, 39–36, 40; *Trin.* VIII, 4, 6.

13. See *Doc.* I, 35, 39–40, 44; *Doc.* III, 10, 14.

14. See the collection D. W. H. Arnold and P. Bright (eds.), *De Doctrina Christiana: A Classic of Western Culture*, Notre Dame, IN 1995, the bibliography by the present author in that volume, 160–75; R. A. Markus, *Signs and Meanings: World and Text in Ancient Christianity*, Liverpool 1996, esp. chs. 1 and 4.

15. For what I mean here by 'attention' see my 'On Teaching Christian Doctrine', *Gregorianum* 79, 1998 (forthcoming).

16. This assertion can easily be tested by reading chs. 6 and 8 of Daley, *The Hope of the Early Church*.

17. See S. L. Cook, *Prophecy and Apocalypticism: The Post-Exilic Social Setting*, Minneapolis, MN 1995.

The Mystery of the Year 1000

Damian Thompson

In the spring of the year 1000, a community of monks in Lotharingia were celebrating the passion and resurrection of the Lord when they felt the whole earth 'shake with a vast and general tremor'. A comet appeared in the sky and hung there for three months. 'It shone so brightly that its light seemed to fill the greater part of the sky,' wrote one contemporary. No one knew exactly what caused it, he added, but this phenomenon never appeared 'without being the sure sign of some mysterious and terrible event. And indeed a fire soon consumed the church of St Michael the Archangel, built on a promontory in the ocean, which had always been the object of special veneration throughout the whole world.'[1]

Fire in the heavens and on earth: no wonder people believed the Last Judgment was at hand. For centuries, the millennial comet was cited by historians in support of their theory that Christendom lived through the year 999 in a state of mortal fear, convinced that, with the completion of a thousand years since the birth of Christ, history had run its course. 'The Terrors of the Year 1000' were believed to have inspired thousands of people to hurry to Jerusalem to witness the Second Coming. 'They were compared to a desolating army,' wrote one nineteenth-century historian. 'Knights, citizens and serfs travelled eastwards . . . looking with fearful eyes upon the sky, which they expected each moment to open, to let the Son of God descend in his glory.'[2] Back home, rich men surrendered wagon-loads of jewels. Convicts were let out of prison. According to one modern popular author, there was even a wave of suicides by those who could not stand the pressure of waiting for the Last Judgment.[3] The nineteenth-century French historian Michelet believed that the end was awaited with as much excitement as fear: 'The captive expected it in his gloomy dungeon. The serf expected it whilst tracing the furrow under the shadow of his lord's hated tower . . . Nor could that moment be without its charm, when the shrill and withering trump of the archangel should peal in the ear of their tyrants. For then, from dungeon, cloister and from furrow, one tremendous shriek of laughter would burst forth from the stricken and oppressed.'[4]

In the event, however, the only shrieks of laughter have been the derisive ones of the twentieth-century historians. For there were no Terrors of the Year 1000, it seems. It is a romantic invention, dating back no further than the sixteenth century. Indeed, some modern historians – especially the French Marxists who once dominated the field – feel it is beneath their dignity even to mention the millennium, except perhaps in a contemptuous footnote. In their lofty view, it demeans the men and women of the late tenth century to suggest that they expected the end of time at the millennium of Christ's birth: they had far more important matters on their mind, such as the evolution of feudal structures. In the words of one French historian, 'it is necessary to wring the neck of this legend'.[5]

In theory, at least, this should not be difficult. It is an undeniable fact that, among the limited range of documents which survives from the late tenth and early eleventh century, *not one makes a reference to widespread fear of the world ending in the year 1000.* On the contrary, the only writer who links the Second Coming to the year 1000 does so only to dismiss the notion. The theologian Abbo of Fleury, writing in 995, recalls that he heard a sermon preached in Paris around the year 960 in which the preacher announced that 'as soon as the number of a thousand years was completed, the Antichrist would come and the Last Judgment would follow soon', an argument which the impeccably orthodox Abbo was easily able to demolish by quoting scripture.[6]

For the truth is that nowhere in the Gospels or Revelation is it stated or implied that the Second Coming will occur a thousand years after the nativity. Throughout Christian history, the most commonly accepted view among apocalyptic believers has been that the millennium, the thousand-year reign of the saints described in Revelation, will begin *after* the Second Coming. Admittedly, this was not the teaching of the church at the end of the tenth century; but it did not sanction the rival theory known as postmillennialism, in which Christ comes at the end of the thousand years, either. Catholic teaching was, and is, based on that of St Augustine, who taught that the reference to a thousand years was purely figurative. According to many historians, therefore, the absence of millennial terrors should not surprise us, since the sole religious authority in the West explicitly opposed any attempt to unveil the time of the End. The peasant or nobleman who cowered in church on 31

December 999 would therefore have been advertising his own hetero-doxy.

But even if there were scriptural foundation for believing that Christ would return on 1 January 1000, many modern authorities are convinced that the date would have passed without incident, for the simple reason that the vast majority of people did not know what year it was. The AD system was far from universal; most educated people still dated current events by regnal years. In any case, it was all a matter of supreme unconcern to the tenth-century peasant, whose existence was governed entirely by the unalterable progression of the seasons. For him, and for most historians, the year 1000 was 'a year like any other'.

And yet, as the third Christian millennium approaches, the neck of the Legend of the Year 1000 remains unwrung. The shelves of bookshops are overflowing with popular books of millennial prophecy, many of which describe peasants and their masters trembling in churches. Stephen Skinner's *Millennium Prophecies* waxes eloquent on the subject. 'December [999] saw fanaticism reach new heights as communities attempted to rid their area of the ungodly so that the Angel of Judgment would not need to call,' it says. 'Bands of flagellants roamed the countryside; mobs called for the execution of supposed sorcerers or unpopular burghers, and even some farm animals were freed to roam through the towns, giving a slightly surrealistic air to the proceedings.'[7] In fact, these are the historical equivalent of urban myths; but, like the vanishing hitchhiker and the poodle in the microwave, they have taken on a life of their own. No dinner-party conversation about the millennium is complete without a prediction that the world is about to experience mass convulsions 'just like it did last time'.

Historians opposed to an apocalyptic reading of the year 1000 can, of course, afford to dismiss these claims; indeed, they enjoy setting the record straight. But what they do not enjoy, and even seem to resent, is any attempt by their fellow academics to challenge the orthodox view of 1000 as 'a year like any other'. Nevertheless, as the millennial anniversary draws closer, that is what is happening.

Since the late 1980s, a number of younger historians have floated the possibility of a year 1000 which was highly charged with apocalyptic significance. While accepting that the romantic picture of the terrors is essentially a myth, they argue that the millennia of Christ's birth in 1000 and resurrection in 1033 were the defining moments in the history of the period. For them, the strange events of those years, such as the vast peace rallies in Southern France and the German Emperor's reinterment of Charlemagne's bones on the feast of Pentecost 1000, must be seen in an apocalyptic light. As for the absence of contemporary references to the significance of the date, that can be compared to the dog which did not bark in the night-time: it is a curious incident which may point to a conspirary of silence.

On one point, however, everyone can agree, and that is the importance of the period in determining the shape of the world we know today. Yet we know relatively little about it. Guy Bois calls the era 'one of the most mysterious in our history'.[8] Felipe Fernandez-Armesto considers the Latin West to be 'perhaps the least civilized civilization of a thousand years ago' in comparison with those of Asia and eastern Christendom.[9] Was Europe still in the Dark Ages? The documents send out conflicting signals. *Servi* and *ancillae* straight out of a Latin primer work alongside that quintessential mediaeval figure, the villein. There is a disorientating quality to the landscape: Viking emissaries wander through Byzantium, like extras who have strayed on to the wrong set; Russian Christians are auctioned off as slaves in Muslim Spain.

In retrospect, Europe was clearly on the verge of the Middle Ages. The linguistic frontier between France and Germany was taking shape. In Northern France, the feudal system was as well established as it was two centuries later. A monastic revival was under way. The year 1000 saw the conversion of Iceland. In the East, the rulers of the Ukraine and Hungary had just been baptized. Underlying these events, meanwhile, was a steady growth in population which would form the basis of mediaeval economic growth.

But the inhabitants of Europe in the year 1000 would not, of course, have been able to foresee the economic boom of the flowering of culture we associate with the Middle Ages. On the contrary, there was a widespread feeling that the world was sliding irrevocably into chaos. The last years of the tenth century saw terrifying Danish raids on England and anarchy and famine in France. To contemporaries, one obvious explanation presented itself: that the world was entering the reign of the Antichrist.

The terrors of the year 1000 might be a myth, but there can be no denying the sense of doom which permeates so many documents of the period. In England, the sermons of Wulfstan, Archbishop of York, refer frequently to the Antichrist in their exhortations to repentance before the Day of Judgment. In France, political collapse persuaded many that society had entered a terminal crisis. 'With the world coming to an end, since men are driven by a briefer life, so does a more atrocious cupidity burn in them,' wrote a monk at St Hilaire of Poitiers in around 995. A similar observation was made by Ralph Glaber, the gossipy Burgundian monk whose *Histories* are one of the most important sources for events in Western Europe at the millennium. Describing the events of the 990s, Glaber argues that the growing wickedness of the clergy is an apocalyptic sign. 'When the piety of bishops wanes . . . does it not seem as if the whole of mankind is sliding back of its own free will into the old abyss of perdition?'[10] (Nearly a thousand years later, incidentally, delegates at an evangelical conference in London argued that the 'apostasy' of the former Bishop of Durham was a sign of the End.)[11]

It is one thing, however, to show that apocalyptic feelings were running high; quite another to prove that this was because the millennium was about to end. But this is exactly what the revisionist school of historians has set out to do. The chief advocate of this view is Professor Richard Landes, director of the Center for Millennial Studies at Boston University, who argues that the Catholic Church was chiefly concerned to ensure that its calendar could not be used to trigger an apocalyptic panic. Hence the complete absence of sources explicitly linking the apocalypse and the Anno Domini calendar. For a cleric to have dwelt on the eschatological significance of the date 1000 would have been foolhardy and even dangerous. And yet, says Landes, if we read between the lines of contemporary accounts, a powerful subliminal message emerges. Despite everything the church could do to play down their significance, both the millennium of Christ's birth and that of his death thirty-three years later were seen by all levels of society as part of an unfolding apocalyptic drama.[12]

Ralph Glaber's testimony is crucial. He describes his *Histories*, written in the 1030s, as 'the story of the events and prodigies which happened around and after the millennial year of the Incarnation of the Saviour'. When he comes to describe the various disasters which occurred in the decade before the year 1000, he dates them with reference to that year. 'In the seventh year from the millennium,' he says, 'almost all the cities of Italy and Gaul were devastated by violent conflagrations.' Soon afterwards, many eminent men died. The impression that these calamities are connected to the approach of the millennium is reinforced when Glaber refers briefly to an outbreak of heresy in Sardinia. 'All this accords with the prophecy of St John, who said that the devil would be freed after a thousand years,' he says.[13] This is a fascinating comment which, taken in conjunction with Abbo's story of the sermon, seems to confirm the existence of a popular belief in the end of the world at the millennium.

Glaber then moves to the year 1003, when something miraculous happens: 'Just before the third year after the millennium, throughout the whole world, but especially in Italy and Gaul, men began to reconstruct churches . . . It was as if the whole world were shaking itself, shrugging off the burden of the past, and cladding itself everywhere in a white mantle of churches.'[14]

There is something very distinctive about this chain of events: disasters, mysterious portents, and a sense of all things made new. Its shape is not unlike that of the ultimate apocalyptic drama foretold in scripture, in which the world falls into chaos before the Second Coming. Richard Landes, for one, is not prepared to accept that the dawn of a Christian millennium in the middle of these events is a coincidence. Moreover, he points out that when another millennium occurs – that of Christ's death in 1033 – the drama of the year 1000 seems to repeat itself. As Glaber puts it: 'After the many prophecies which had broken upon the world, before, after and around the millennium of the Lord Christ, there were plenty of able men of penetrating intellect who foretold others, just as great, at the approach of the millennium of the Lord's Passion, and such wonders were soon manifest.' This time around, a famine forces men to eat potters clay and wolves gorge on the dead. 'Men feared that the orderly procession of the seasons . . . had relapsed into eternal chaos; and they feared that mankind would end,' said Glaber, who now uses the year 1033 to set the date. Heresy breaks out among the Lombards and the roads to Jerusalem fill up with pilgrims. Asked why this is happening, the 'more truthful of that time . . . cautiously responded that it presaged nothing else but the coming of the Lost One, the Antichrist, who according to divine authority stands ready to come at the End of the Age'.[15]

Finally, Glaber's description of the 1030 millennium conjures up a picture of a relieved population offering thanks for the renewal of creation. 'At the millennial anniversary of the passion of the Lord, the clouds cleared in obedience to divine mercy and goodness, and the smiling sky began to shine and blow gentle breezes,' he says. 'At that point, in the region of Aquitaine, bishops, abbots and other men devoted to holy religion first began to gather councils of the whole people . . . When the news of these assemblies was heard, the entire populace joyfully came, unanimously prepared to follow whatever should be commanded them by the pastors of the church.'[16]

Glaber is describing something called the 'Peace of God': a movement of popular revulsion against warring noblemen which was initiated by the clergy and lasted for several decades. Landes believes that the Peace of God, whose early phrase lasted from the 990s until the

1033s, bears the stamp of an authentic millenarian movement. To understand the peace councils, he says, we need to grasp the dynamics of apocalyptic behaviour. His study of events in Limoges in 994, when in response to an outbreak of 'fire plague' the bishop, abbot and duke called a three-day fast followed by a council, suggests a classic millenarian sequence. First, there was a disaster. The plague was possibly an outbreak of ergotism, a hallucinogenic poison which appeared with the spread of rye cultivation; it can affect whole communities, producing visions 'from atrocious visions of hell to ecstatic ones of heaven', and indeed did so in France as recently as the 1950s. This was followed by a mass terror and guilt, public acts of repentance, a miracle producing euphoria and, finally, an alliance of peace and justice mutually sworn by all the lords present.

Now compare this to Ralph Glaber's vivid description of a council in 1033, at which, following extraordinary miracles, 'the bishops raised their staffs towards heaven and all present stretched their palms to God, shouting with one voice "Peace! Peace!"'.[17] This sounds suspiciously like millennial fervour. There is no sense of terror, but then people who expect an immediate apocalypse often act constructively and energetically. It is a strange fact that apocalyptic disappointment can produce a great surge of energy – enough, perhaps to produce a 'white mantle of churches' in recognition of the fact that mankind has passed its moment of danger and has entered a new millennium.

Another striking clue to the apocalyptic significance of the year 1000 lies in the mysterious behaviour of the young Emperor Otto III, which is hard to understand except as an imagined end-time drama. The Ottonians were obsessed with the idea of ruling a reincarnated Roman Empire. Otto, who was half Saxon and half Greek by birth, took over the reins of power in 994 at the age of fourteen. He had been brought up among clerics who were fascinated by the Book of Revelation, and in a court which took very seriously the tradition of Rome as the last and greatest world empire.

Just before the millennium, Otto seized control of Rome. He adopted a seal which included the words *Renovatio imperii Romanorum*; the implication was that, under him, the history of the world had reached its glorious apogee. In the year 1000, Otto visited Charlemagne's capital of Aachen. 'He was in doubt where the bones of Charlemagne lay,' records the chronicler Thietmar. 'So he had the floor [of the Basilica] secretly breached, and ordered workmen to dig where he thought they were. In due course the bones were found seated on the royal throne. Otto removed the golden cross which hung on Charles's neck, and such of the clothes as had not crumbled to dust, and the rest were reinterred with great devotion.'[18] This reburial, which took place on the feast of Pentecost, is clearly a symbolic event; and it becomes even more so when we remember that Charlemagne was crowned in a year, 800, which at the time was believed to mark the beginning of the seventh and final thousand-year period in history. For the Emperor of the year 1000 to have paid tribute to the Emperor of the year 6000 at such a juncture draws attention to a powerful symmetry. But, given the hostility of the Church to date-setting, it could not be officially acknowledged or explained.

The Emperor would have been well aware of the approach of the fateful year 1000. There remains, though, the awkward question of how many ordinary people would have had access to this information – and, if so, whether they would have cared. The apocalyptic and anti-apocalyptic schools differ on this point. The former insist that the Anno Domini calendar was extremely well established in the monasteries of Western Europe: anyone who came into contact with monks would have been in a position to establish the AD date. But the anti-apocalyptic scholars point out that the whole notion of 'date' had not fully developed by this stage; and, in any case, there was no consensus as to when the year began. New Year's Day fell on 1 January in many places, but in Rome at Christmas, in Florence on 25 March, in Venice on 1 March and in France at Easter.[19]

But was it necessary to think in terms of calendars and dates to be aware of the onset of the millennium? We are in danger of imposing an anachronistic understanding of time on an earlier society. The millennium was not synonymous with 'entering a new century', a meaningless concept at the time. From reading Glaber, it seems clear that what mattered about all was the simple fact that a thousand years had elapsed since the Saviour's birth. From this it followed that the next thirty-three years would witness the millennium of the life of Christ, culminating in the glorious anniversary of his resurrection. Judging by the crowds shouting 'Peace! Peace!' in the fields of France, the beginning and end of this period aroused expectations of a new heaven and a new earth; and the same may be true of the pilgrims who rushed to Jerusalem in 1033. In contrast, though, there must have been many people – in areas where the Anno Domini calendar was not established, such as the fringes of the West and most of eastern Christendom – for whom the year 1000 really was a year like any other.

It seems likely, though, that the millennial experiences of most people lay somewhere in between these extremes. On the first page of his *Histories*, Glaber talks about 'many events which occurred with unusual frequency about the millennium of the Incarnation of Christ our Saviour', without explaining *why* they happened more often at this time. This is probably because he did not know why: although he implies that there was a connection between these interesting times and the millennium, he does not presume to understand God's purpose. Other documents of the period hint at popular feelings of anxiety or fear before both millennial anniversaries, and celebration or relief after them; but these are neither explained nor described in any detail. This may be because the authors, who were almost all monks, were forbidden to speculate on such matters. But it may also be because they could not fully account for such feelings. And if that is the case, then the gap between our perceptions of our own millennium and those of the men and women of a thousand years ago is perhaps not so great after all.

[A longer version of this article appears in Damian Thompson's book *The End of Time: Faith and Fear in the Shadow of the Millennium*, Sinclair-Stevenson, London 1996; University Press of New England 1997.]

Notes

1. R. Glaber, *Histories*, Book III, Ch. 3, Rodulfus Glaber Opera, ed. J. France, Oxford 1989.

2. C. Mackay, *Memoirs of Extraordinary Popular Delusions and the Madness of Crowds*, London 1852, 257–8.

3. C. Berlitz, *Doomsday 1999 AD*, New York 1981, 9–12.

4. J. Michelet, *History of France*, London 1844, 143–4.

5. F. Lot, 'Le mythe des Terreurs de l'an Mille', *Mercure de France*, 1947, 300.

6. Abbo, *Liber apologeticus*, quoted in H. Focillon, *The Year 1000*, London 1970, 54.

7. S. Skinner, *Millennium Prophecies*, London 1994, 69.

8. G. Bois, *The Transformation of the Year One Thousand*, Manchester 1992, 1.

9. F. Fernandez-Armesto, *Millennium*, New York 1995, 47.

10. Glaber, *Histories* (n. 1), II, 12.

11. Conference on the Second Coming organized by Time Ministries at High Leigh, Herts, attended by the author, November 1994.

12. R. Landes, 'The Apocalyptic Year 1000', in *The Year 2000: Essays on the End*, ed. Strozier and Flynn, New York 1997.

13. Glaber, *Histories* (n. 1), V, 1.

14. Ibid, II, 12.

15. Ibid, III, 13.

16. Ibid, IV, 5.

17. Ibid, IV, 4–6.

18. Thietmar, quoted in C. Brooke, *Europe in the Central Middle Ages*, London 1987, 226.

19. H. Schwartz, *Century's End: A Cultural History of the Fin de Siecle from the 990s through the 1990s*, New York 1990, 28.

III · Scientific Perspectives

The Mortality of the Planet

Kenneth J. Hsu

Venus is dead. With surface temperature now more than 600°C, the planet is an inferno of fire. Mars is dead. With surface temperature colder than 100°C below freezing, even carbon dioxide is frozen to make dry ice. There are no rivers, no lakes, no oceans; there is no water to sustain life on Mars. Our planet is alive, populated with living organisms for the last 3.5 billion years at least. Earth has always been alive since then. With oceans that never boiled nor completely froze to the bottom, life on Earth has never been completely exterminated. The surface temperature on planets depends upon (1) solar radiation received, (2) solar radiation lost through reflection from the planetary surface – the albedo effect, (3) reflected solar radiation trapped by greenhouse gases (such as carbon dioxide and methane) in the planetary atmosphere – the greenhouse effect.

Solar input was weaker in the beginning, but the solar radiation increased logarithmically some three billion years ago, and became more or less constant during the last two billion years. The albedo effect is unpredictable. There could be a positive-feedback mechanism: it has been found, for example, that years of early snow will have colder winters because of the amount of heat reflected by the snow-covered ground. There have been, however, no systematic variations of the albedo effect in earth history, nor systematic climatic changes attributable to a variable albedo effect. Scientists have thus related planetary temperatures to the so-called greenhouse effect, and the long-range history of climate on planets has been interpreted in terms of varying concentration of the greenhouse gases in the atmosphere.

On Venus more carbon dioxide from the planetary interior has been released to the Venusian stratosphere than escaped from the gravitational hold of the planet. Accumulating over billions of years, Venus is enveloped in a dense atmosphere of carbon dioxide, and the planet has become an inferno of fire.

The concentration of greenhouse gases on Earth's atmosphere has been variable, because there has been life on earth. A living organism is alive when it makes sugar out of carbon dioxide and water, with phosphorous as a catalyst. After the organism dies, the dead body decays to form carbon dioxide and water again, releasing phosphorous. A best-selling author pointed out the obvious: Gaia converts carbon dioxide and water into a chemistry professor, and the chemistry professor after his demise returns the carbon dioxide and water to Gaia. In a perfect carbon-recycling process, as much carbon dioxide is returned as has been utilized by living organisms. At the same time, the planet's atmosphere should get increasingly enriched by the carbon dioxide released by volcanoes. The recycling by living organisms has not, however, been perfect: part of life is fossilized, after death, as a carbon-compound. In coastal swamps, for example, plant remains are carbonized. On tidal flats, cyanobacteria form algal mats and they precipitate carbon as calcium carbonate. The carbon-fixation process is a most common sedimentary process on Earth: the carbon from dead plants makes coal, and the mineral precipitated by cyanobacteria makes limestone.

Geochemical evidence indicates that there has never been too much nor too little carbon dioxide in the terrestrial atmosphere. James Lovelock postulates that the living organisms on Earth provide a feedback mechanism to adjust the level. Such a self-organizing system has been given the metaphor Gaia. The Earth is not a fireball, Lovelock believes, because the interaction of living organisms and their environments is a self-organizing system adjusting the concentration of greenhouse gases in the atmosphere.

In a talk delivered at the British Association for the Advancement of Science, I found similarities when I compared the carbon-cycling on Earth to money-circulation in a market-economy. More money in circulation causes inflation. An increase in the interest rate discourages borrowing and thus serves to lock up some money in the Federal Reserve Bank to effect deflation. A deflation can lead to recession or even to a great depression. The bank thus intervenes wisely, and lowers the interest rate at the proper moment to again inflate the economy. Paraphrasing the economic phrases with scientific jargon, followers of the 'Gaia sect' have been saying: more carbon dioxide in the atmosphere causes a rise of planetary temperature. The evolution of organisms such as plants causes the burial of fossil carbon and thus removes some atmospheric carbon dioxide to effect a decrease of global temperature.

The decrease can eventually lead to an ice age, or to even the mortality of the planet. Gaia, however, has always intervened, and caused, at the proper moment, the evolution of other forms of organisms which effectively release fossil carbon as carbon dioxide into the atmosphere, so as to increase the global temperature again through greenhouse warming. This is the essence of my paper 'Is Gaia Endothermic?', in which I related the history of terrestrial climate to biological evolution (Hsu, 1994).

Venus is dead. If there ever was life, the Venusian organisms were not sufficiently efficient to take enough volcanic carbon dioxide out of the planetary carbon-cycling. Venus was to get steadily hotter, and any life that might have been there was to be exterminated.

Mars is dead, but there may have been life on Mars billions of years ago. Scientists believe that the earliest forms of life on earth are thermophilic bacteria, like those found today in hot thermal vents on top of submarine volcanoes on the floor of the Pacific Ocean. The earliest Martian life was probably also some form of bacteria. They took carbon dioxide from the Martian atmosphere, and after their death, the carbon dioxide did not return completely, at least, not as much as would have been necessary to keep the carbon-dioxide concentration of the Martian atmosphere in a quasi-steady state. The carbon dioxide was then reduced to such an extent that its greenhouse effect became insufficient to keep Mars warm enough to prevent the freezing of the planet, when life could no longer be sustained.

Mars most probably died some three billion years ago, when the solar energy radiated by the Sun was only a fraction of what it is now. At that time, the greenhouse gases on the planets should have been hundreds of times more concentrated to keep the planets from freezing. Without an effective protection by greenhouse gases, Mars became mortal. How did Earth escape the fate of Mars?

Classifying on the basis whether living organisms on Earth tend to bury or release more greenhouse gases to the atmosphere, there are only two kinds: the 'heaters' and the 'air-conditioners' (Hsu, 1994). The dominant life on Earth three billion yeas ago was bacteria, thermophilic and/or anerobic, and those were 'air-conditioners': a part of their dead bodies, however small, was fossilized so that the atmospheric carbon dioxide kept on decreasing. Earth was going the way of Mars, when Gaia intervened: she saw to it that a heater-organism evolved. The 'heater' consisted of methanogenic bacteria. These single-cell creatures eat carbonate mineral, converting it into methane, and this hydrocarbon is a greenhouse gas, molecule for molecule four times more effective than carbon dioxide. Studying the isotope geochemistry of ancient rocks, geologists found that methanogenic bacteria were indeed a dominant fossil-organism during the interval 2.9 to 2.5 billion years ago. Their release of methane was to keep the Earth warm enough to sustain life. One can speculate that the evolution of life on Mars never progressed to the stage of methanogenic bacteria, so that the planet died.

The history of terrestrial climate since then is a continuing record of the alternating dominance of 'air-conditioners' and 'heaters'. When our planet was again over-heated some two billion years ago, Gaia gave us cyanobacteria, an 'air-conditioner', because it precipitates carbon dioxide as carbonate in limestone. This new life form was the dominant life form until some 650 million years ago, when the over-zealous 'air-conditioner' was about to turn the Earth into an icebox. Gaia had to act, and the next new life forms were soft-bodied animals: worms, medusas, etc. They ate up cyanobacteria, and gave back to the atmosphere the carbon-dioxide and water which were taken, so that the greenhouse gas in the atmosphere could increase again through the emanations from volcanoes. Cyanobacteria were a kind of 'heater', and the climate on earth was ameliorated. Organisms with carbonate skeletons evolved some 550 million years ago, and they partially replaced soft-bodied animals. Later, some 350 million years ago, swamp plants evolved and their carbonization was to again refrigerate the planet. The over-zealous 'air-conditioners' caused their own extermination: coal-making tropical plants did not survive the Ice Age. Tundra and desert plants took over, and their carbon was not fossilized. Replenished by volcanic gases, the planet's atmosphere again became an adequate greenhouse. Eventually the planet became so warm that there were no polar ice caps some 200 million years ago. The warm oceans often became stagnant, and the toxic bottom became uninhabitable for marine benthos. Gaia had to do something.

The next great event in the history of terrestrial life was the evolution of flowering plants and of calcareous planktons, which are floating one-celled organisms with a carbonate skeleton. They were the new 'air-conditioners', and their work brought us to the most recent Ice Age.

Hominids evolved some five or six million years ago, when the Antarctic ice cap had reached its greatest extent, and when the Arctic glaciation was about to begin. Our species, *Homo sapiens*, evolved some 50,000 years ago, when northern Eurasia and North America were buried in ice. The species multiplied towards the end of the Ice Age, and our civilization has evolved to burn fossil fuel to warm up the Earth. We are

Gaia's 'heaters', but are we to trigger a 'greenhouse catastrophe' to cause our own extinction or even to cause the mortality of our planet?

We need to look back into the past to predict the future. Studies by paleoclimatologists, earth scientists, astronomers and historians have all shown that the terrestrial climate has not been the same since the last retreat of the continental glaciers some 10,000 years ago. There was a 'climatic optimum' for about five millenia, but the good climate ended rather abruptly 4000 BP (before present), when the Sahara again became a desert and when glaciers came back to the Alps.

The fact is that factors other than the greenhouse effect can influence the terrestrial climate. The solar energy received by the Earth is approximately, but not precisely, constant. When Earth's orbital motion brings it farthest from the Sun, the energy-input is the least. Scientists have found that alternations of the glacial advances and retreats of the last Ice Age are precisely correlated to the cyclicities of the planetary motion. The durations of those cycles of 100,000, 40,000 and 20,000 years have been recorded by ocean sediments laid down over two million years. There are, furthermore, shorter climatic cycles, too short and not precisely periodic enough to reflect the planetary orbital motion, and these quasi-periodic changes of solar input range from ten to eleven years (sun-spot cycles) to about 1200 or 1300 years (Perry, 1989). The global temperature of our planet during the last 150 years is not correlative to the greenhouse effect, but best correlated to the duration of sun-spot cycles (Friis-Christensen and Lassen, 1991). I have found evidence that the terrestrial climate during the last 10,000 years is best correlated to the 1200-year solar cycles (Hsu, 1998).

Work by our laboratory in the early 1990s discovered the global synchroneity of the termination of the climatic optimum during the centuries around 2000 BC. Global cooling caused the shift of precipitation from low/middle latitudes to high latitudes. The Sahara had been a country of great lakes during the climatic optimum: people fished in rivers and lakes, and palms grew on sandy shores (Petit-Mayer and Riser, 1983). Global cooling caused a weakening of monsoons from the West African tropical waters, so that the Sahara became a desert. This same pattern of climatic change was, in fact, observed during the 1960/70s, when the Sahel suffered its worst drought (Bryson and Murray, 1977). In the Near East, Mesopotamia had been a great farming country. The global chill caused a period of aridity there which lasted some 300 years, when the villages and cities were abandoned. At about the same time, the Indus Valley civilization collapsed and Egypt declined (Weiss et al., 1993).

Global cooling brought more precipitation to central and northern Europe. Mountain glaciers came back to the Alps. Rains and melting snows caused abrupt flooding in lowlands when the Lake-Dwellers had to abandon their settlements (Jacomet et al., 1995). Cattle-farming became all but impossible, with cold and wet summers. The Indo-Europeans of northern Germany and southern Scandinavia had to move south, with their corded-ware pottery and their battle axes, to find better pastures: they went to southern Russia, from there to south-eastern Europe, to Anatolia, to Persia and India, and to north-west China (Kossina, 1902; Mair, 1996; Hsu, 1997).

The amelioration of the terrestrial climate came after a few hundred years, and global warming was a blessing to societies based upon agricultural economy. The great civilizations of Egypt and Mesopotamia flowered during the Late Bronze Age. In China, the great Shang Empire was established on the northern plains of China (Liu, 1982; Hsu, 1995).

The second global chill of historical time came during the few centuries before and after 800 BC. It was so cold on the shores of the Baltic Sea that people changed the way they spoke: the open-mouthed vowels a, o, u, were replaced by the closed mouthed Umlaut ä, ö, ü (Pokorny, 1936). Many had to leave their home and became the Dorian Invaders, and the 'People of the Sea' described by biblical scholars (Keller, 1956). Lake-Dwellers of central Europe, who had returned to build new settlements on lake shores during the warm interlude, were forced again to flee (Jacomet et al., 1995). Farther south, the climate was cold and arid, and that was the dark age of the Mediterranean civilization (James, 1991). There are indications that the chill was global. Cold and aridity caused crop failures and famines, leading to the decline and disintegration of the great Zhou Empire of China at about 800 BC (Liu, 1982).

The next warm interlude saw the Golden Age of the Greeks in the West and of the Warring States in the East, followed by the Roman and Han Empires (Hsu, 1996). The southern shores of the Baltic were inhabited by Germanic tribes, and the Iron-Age Celtic people came to settle on the shores of central European lakes (Jacomet et al., 1995; Hsu, 1996).

The next global chill in the first centuries after the birth of Christ may have been the worst in history. Historical documents in China recorded the coldest climate and the most severe droughts ever during the fourth century: after two arid periods each lasting some forty years, people could wade across the Yellow and Yangtze Rivers (Liu, 1982). Many farming families had to move to south China, where they cut down the forests for rice fields. Deprived of a sound economic base, the Chinese who stayed behind were no match for the northern invaders. The Han Dynasty disintegrated, and the 'Five Barbarian Nations' brought chaos to north and central China (Hsu, 1995; 1996).

In the West, the global chill was an ultimate cause of the Migrations of the German Nations (Hsu, 1996). Goths, Vandals, Burgunders, Alemans, Lombards and other German tribes on the shores of the Baltic moved south during the second, third and fourth centuries when the cold and wet climate prevailed (Alföldi, 1967; Wolfram, 1979). Farmers had to leave, so that Northern Europe became sparsely populated; only fishers remained in coastal villages. The East Goths settled in southern Russian and the West Goths, Vandals, and others in central Europe during the third and fourth centuries, before the Huns came and Attila drove the Germanic tribes to 'wander' all across Europe (Hsu, 1997). The Roman Empire fell in AD 476.

Hardship forced people to improvise. North America had been populated by hunters and gatherers. Now the natural produce of the land was no longer sufficient, North American Indians learned to farm, and their descendants were to become the Anasazis (Cordell, 1984). In Central America, however, the global chill was apparently a blessing. Tropical jungles could be cleared for farm lands, and the Mayans rose to build a great civilization (Coe, 1994).

Sunny climate 'came back' to northern Europe during the sixth or seventh century. Slavic farmers moved from the east into the 'no man's land' between the Elbe and the Oder. The Germans moved back later, from the west, in the name of Christianization after the ninth century. They pushed the Slavs back, and the *Drang nach Osten* (push to the east) continued until the defeat of Nazi Germany in World War II. The warmer climate permitted the Scandinavians to extend their farms northward beyond the Arctic Circle, and the greening of the north caused a population explosion. Over-populated, some Vikings made their raids south, and established Norman empires in France, Britain, North Africa and Sicily in the tenth, eleventh, and twelfth centuries. Others went west to Iceland and Greenland (Hsu, 1996; 1997). Global warming also caused the greening of desert. The cattle-farming nomadic peoples of northern Asia had an economic base for their conquests. The Huns took over the Tocharian kingdoms of north-west China, and their interbreeding with the Indo-Europeans gave rise to the Turkish race, who first 'appeared' in Chinese history during the seventh century. The Chiangs invaded Tibet, and during the tenth century those staying at home founded the great Xia Kingdom in Ningxia, which is now a desert. The Seljuyk Turks trekked to the west in the eleventh century and took over more and more of Anatolia from Byzantium. The Liaos and Jins came south and occupied the northern Chinese plains. The expansion of the northern Asiatic tribes reached their zenith when Ginghis Khan and his successors conquered everything in sight during the thirteenth century (Hsu, 1997).

Global warming was also a blessing in North America; the warm climate permitted the flowering of the Anasazi culture. The farmers built settlements and cave-dwellings for hundreds or thousands of people during the ninth and thirteenth centuries (Cordell, 1984). While the amelioration of climate made the north more inhabitable, the Mayans, for some reason, abandoned their cities and fields around AD 900 (Coe, 1994). Archaeologists are still debating the cause of their sudden decline. I personally was inspired by a colleague who pointed out the expansion of the habitat of malaria mosquitos during periods of global warming: probably the Mayans had to leave because of malaria epidemics in their homes in tropical lowlands; they went north to Yucatan where malaria mosquitos could not survive (Hsu, 1997).

The last global chill came during the Little Ice Age (Lamb, 1982). Central Europe was a land of misery, devastated by the Thirty Years War. The fact is that the marauding soldiers of Wallenstein were starved peasants; they took up arms when they were allowed to subsist on the harvests of others. Famines, epidemics and infant mortality during the Little Ice Age caused a reduction of the German population from 16 to 9 million people (Hsu, 1997).

The consequence of global cooling in China was equally catastrophic: crops failed eight years in a row, during three of which not a drop of rain fell in central China. Starved mobs stormed state granaries, and the Li Zhicheng gang went all the way to Beijing to force the suicide of the Ming Emperor. After the Manchus re-established order in China, their census indicated a decrease of population from 100 to 30 million (Hsu, 1997).

The hardship of the Little Ice Age caused the rise of the national states. In Europe, Spain, France, England and Holland embarked on a colonial policy and shifted their economy from an agricultural to a mercantile and eventually an industrial basis (Kennedy, 1989). There were crop failures in Great Britain during the cold and wet years, but they could buy crops with the cash surplus from trade. Furthermore, their starving farmers could emigrate. In Mexico and South America, the Aztec and Inca peoples founded their empires. They replaced a dependence on agriculture with an organization of communities distributed in different ecological realms. They built roads so that the starving population in one region would be fed by the harvests of another where there were still favourable conditions for farming (Moseley, 1992).

Our planet only came out of the Little Ice Age during the nineteenth century. The warming trend since 1840 was only the beginning, having been interrupted three times during the last 150 years. The last cooling trend during the 1960s and 1970s caused drought and famine in the Sahel Zone, and the publication of books harbingering the inevitable catastrophe of starvation during the next Little Ice Age (Bryson and Murray, 1977; Ponte, 1976).

Lessons of history bring me back to the theme of the mortality of the planet. No, the planet will not die. Gaia will see to it that the species, the destroyer, will become extinct before the Earth itself becomes uninhabitable. This is my faith, and my faith is supported by the record of four billion years of the earth's history.

Will *Homo sapiens* become extinct?

More than 99.9 per cent of the species which ever existed on Earth are now extinct. I find no convincing reason that the species *Homo sapiens* will be an exception. On the other hand, I do not share the sensationalism of some ecologists who envision that the production of industrial carbon dioxide would cause the ocean to boil. That is nonsense.

Global warming during the historical past has been, on the whole, a blessing to mankind, even though there were serious deleterious effects here and there (Hsu, 1996; 1997). Global cooling, on the other hand, has been almost always a catastrophe for societies based upon agricultural economy. Cold and wet climate in the north drove the cattle- and/or crop-farmers away and they became barbarian invaders. At the same time, cold and arid climate in the Mediterranean region and China caused famines and chaos.

Nevertheless, *Homo sapiens* is inventive. We have lived through several cycles of Little Ice Age. We have not only prevailed, but also multiplied. Thanks to human ingenuity, we shall grow enough crops to feed the world's population as long as there is a political awareness of the need for a limitation of population growth. The problem, as I see it, is not climate, but human greed. This is my scenario for a possible mortality of the planet:

We continue with our market economy and our goal of maximalization of profit. We continue to consume our natural resources, including water – the most precious of all commodities. Sooner or later, perhaps as early as the next century, there will be a Little Ice Age. There will be crop failures in northern Europe and more northern parts of North America because of too short a growing season. There will be decimation of cattle in northern and central Europe because of summers too cold and wet for hay-making. There will be famines in the Sahel zone, in the Middle East, in the Indus Valley, and in China because of droughts. The grains produced from the rest of the world spared the catastrophic consequences of a global chill may be sufficient to feed the world population, if people share. Are we to share or are we to take from others? Lessons of greed from history are not encouraging.

Shortage of water will be the most critical problem. During the Little Ice Age of the East Jin Dynasty, the Chinese moved south, subjugated the indigenous population, and deforested virgin land to make rice fields. During the Little Ice Age towards the end of the Ming Dynasty, there was no more virgin land in the south to be deforested. Starving farmers roved around the countryside, robbing the others and bringing down the imperial dynasty. If there should be another Little Ice Age, where will the starving peasants go? There are a billion Chinese who live on their land. When the land yields no produce, they will have to start marauding the countryside as their ancestors did repeatedly during the historical past. There could be a half-billion boat people. Or the peasants could join the People's Liberation Army and march into South-East Asia, where there is much water but little surplus land.

An invasion on such a scale is a cause for war. How are we to prevent the warring parties in their desperation from using nuclear weapons? Could *Homo sapiens* survive a nuclear holocaust? Is a world infected by radioactivity still inhabitable for any living organisms?

The mortality of our planet will not be due to natural causes, thanks to the grace of God. The mortality of our planet could be brought about by the greed of our species, when even Gaia could not save us.

Bibliography

Alfoldi, Andreas, 1967, *Studien zur Geschichte der Weltkrise des dritten Jahrhunderts nach Christus*, Darmstadt, cited by Wolfram, 1988.

Bryson, R. A. and Murray, T. J., 1977, *Climates of Hunger*, Madison, Wisc.

Coe, M. D., 1994, *Mexico, from the Olmecs to the Aztecs*, fourth edition, London.

Cordell, L. S., 1984, *Prehistory of the Southwest*, San Diego.

Friis-Christensen, Eigel, and Lassen, Knud, 1991, 'Correlation of global temperature to sunspot cycles', *Science* 254, 698.

Hsu, K. J., 1992, 'Is Gaia Endothermic?', *Geological Magazine* 129, 129–41.

——, 1966, 'Could global warming be a blessing for mankind?', *Terrestrial, Atmospheric and Oceanic Science* 8, Taiwan, 375–92.

——, 1997a, 'Did the Xinjiang Indo-Europeans leave their home because of global cooling?', in Mair, V. H. (ed.), *The Bronze Age and Early Iron Age People of Eastern Central Asia* (forthcoming).

——, 1997b, 'Sun, climate, hunger, and mass migrations', *Chinese Science Bulletin* 42, Beijing (forthcoming).

Jacomet, S., Magny, M., and Burga, C. A., 1995, 'Klima- und Seespiegelschwankungen im Verlauf des Neolithikums und ihre Auswirkungen auf die Besiedlung der Seeüfer', in *Die Schweiz von Paläolithikum bis zum frühen Mittelalter*, Basel, 53–8.

Keller, W., 1956, *The Bible as History*, London and New York.

Kennedy, Paul, 1987, *The Rise and Fall of the Great Powers*, New York and London.

Kossina, G., 1902, 'Die indogermanische Frage archäologisch beantwortet', in A. Scherer (ed.) *Die Urheimat der Indogermanen*, Darmstadt, 25–109.

James, P., 1991, *Centuries of Darkness*, London.

Lamb, H. H., 1982, *Klima und Kulturgeschichte*, Hamburg.

Liu Shaomin, 1982, *Changing Climate of China in Historical Time*, Taiwan, 76–124.

Mair, Victor H., 1996, 'Progress report for project entitled "A study of the genetic composition of ancient desiccated corpses from Xinjiang (Sinkiang), China"', *Early China News* 6, 1–9.

Moseley, M. E., 1994, *The Incas*, London.

Perry, C. A., 1989, *A Solar Chronometer for Climate*, PhD Diss. Kansas Univ., Lawrence, Kansas.

Petit-Maire, N., and Riser, J., 1983, *Saraha ou Sahel?*, Paris.

Pokorny, Julius, 1936, 'Substrattheorie und Urheimat der Indogermanen', in A. Scherer (ed.), *Die Urheimat der Indogermanen*, Darmstadt, 176–213.

Ponte, L., 1976, *The Cooling*, Englewood Cliffs, NJ.

Weiss, H., Courty, M. A., Wetterstrom, W., Guichard, F., Senior, L., Meadow, R., and Curnow, A., 1993, 'The genesis and collapse of third-millennium north Mesopotamian civilization', *Science* 261, 995–1104.

Wolfram, Herwig, 1988, *History of the Goths*, Berkeley.

The Future of the Universe

Andreas Albrecht and Christopher J. Isham

I. Introduction

This is a very active time in the field of cosmology. On the one hand, terrestrial and satellite-based observations have provided vast new data sets about the detailed large-scale structure of the universe; on the other hand, there have been substantial theoretical developments, particularly concerning the role played by fundamental particle physics in the immediate post-Big-Bang era. This happy confluence of fact and theory has generated an unparalleled excitement in the scientific community, and much has been written on the very early universe and how it is believed to have expanded and developed to produce the world we see today. Even the very origin of the universe has been the subject of intense discussion within the context of 'quantum cosmology' – a suitably esoteric mix of quantum theory and Einstein's general theory of relativity.[1]

In the light of this intense study of the beginning of the universe it is perhaps surprising that so little has been said about how it is all expected to end. To some extent such reservation is justified: the further one looks into the future, the less certain becomes the status and applicability of current scientific knowledge. However, contemplating the 'end of things' can generate deep emotions, with an associated tendency for various non-scientific agenda to become more prominent in proportion to the diminishing quantity of genuine science. For example, there have been highly speculative conjectures about the future of the human race – frequently in the form of triumphalist accounts of how mankind will conquer the entire universe;[2] at the other extreme are the apocalyptic scientific accounts of the inevitable end of the human race, with an implicit challenge to those who seek panentheistic meaning in a universe apparently governed by the physicalist categories of blind chance and the law of increasing entropy.

Notwithstanding the millenarian tendencies of the *fin de siècle* scientists who indulge in such activities, it is clearly of some interest to try to give a balanced scientific account of the anticipated future of the universe in the light of modern cosmology. Such is the focus of this article and, in the process, we explore the boundary between what is known about the universe and what is unknown. However, moderation is indeed required, since it turns out that despite the rapid pace of progress in the field, clear predictions about the future of the universe require information that we do not have, and some of which we could not expect to acquire for another ten billion[3] years at the earliest.

So what does it mean to study the 'future of the universe'? Certainly, the task is a peculiar one. The paradigmatic procedure of science is to formulate a hypothesis about the way things are, which is then tested or falsified by appropriate observations and/or experiments. This is fine for statements about the immediate future – indeed, all predictions of normal science are predictions about the near future of a small part of the universe – but it is clear that claims about the ultimate end of the universe cannot be probed in this way: an observer at this terminal event would experience no time afterwards in which to perform the calculations necessary to confirm or refute his or her predictions; and, anyway, none of us will live anything like long enough.

But problems arise not only in regard to the 'end'. We also have to consider the possibility that the laws of physics contain a temporal component that is as yet unobserved, and hence is unknown to us. In practice, the most that can be done is to make theoretical extrapolations from current data and conceptual frameworks with the hope that existing theory is adequate to cover whatever period of future time we hope to include. Evidently, the problem encountered here is not unrelated to the infamous difficulty of justifying the inductive reasoning of science in general: more specifically, we have to assume that (i) the fundamental mathematical and conceptual laws of physics are not time-dependent in an unpredictable way;[4] and (ii) our current understanding of these timeless laws is sufficient to include all eventualities that might arise in the future.

At the level of theoretical physics, some relief from this problem in the context of the 'end' of things would be obtained if the history of the universe was thought to be described by one of the cyclic solutions[5] to the cosmological equations of general relativity: in this case, the end would be a mirror of the beginning, and could be studied as such. However, the standard view is that – although most of the known fundamental laws of physics are indeed time-symmetric[6] – there is, nevertheless, a marked asymmetry between the initial and the (anticipated) final states of the universe: specifically, the initial conditions of the universe were relatively simple and the universe has been growing in both size and complexity since then.

This brings us inevitably to the 'arrow of time' – something that is likely to feature prominently in any discussion of the beginning or end of the universe. There are several different arrows of time, all of which play some role in our chosen subject. At a psychological level, the feeling of being trapped in an irrevocable movement from the remembered past to an unknown future surely drives mankind's sometimes obsessive quest for material improvement or eschatological meaning as is reflected, for example, in the more manic speculations about the end of the universe alluded to earlier. The psychological arrow of time also determines our view of the scientific method itself, especially the different statuses afforded to prediction and to retrodiction. And, of course, the perceived unidirectional nature of time is deeply involved in the problem of induction and in the general issues concerning the scientific meaning of studies of the future. At a more physical level, the postulated existence of simple cosmological initial conditions – the so-called 'cosmological' arrow of time – underpins the scientific attempts to understand other arrows of time such as the thermodynamic arrow (entropy always increases) or the psychological arrow of the unidirectional flow of experienced time.

II. Four forces of the future

Let us consider now the four related physical processes that seem likely to form the main ingredients in any discussion of the future of the universe: stellar evolution; the constitution of matter; the stability of matter; the force of gravity – especially the formation and decay of black holes.

If – with a familiar hubris – the future of the universe is construed as meaning the future of the human race, then it must be said that although the probability appears to be very low, it is still possible that our entire civilization will be wiped out by an asteroid; or that eventually we will be sucked into a black hole. For that matter, we might destroy ourselves in nuclear or biological warfare. Then there is the predicted end of hydrogen burning in the sun, which will cause the sun to become a 'Red Giant', swelling in size to engulf the earth and thereby vaporizing us all.[7] Any of these events would mark the 'end of the universe' from our point of view. However, from the perspective of the entire observable universe, any such local calamity would be inconsequential: there will always be the odd black hole or emerging red giant, but these events form part of a big picture that is expected to remain remarkably steady over many billions of years.

Turning to the universe at large, here too stellar evolution is of central importance. As a star proceeds along its life cycle, different nuclear fuels are consumed (starting with hydrogen produced in the Big Bang), and different nuclei are produced. This process changes the chemical composition of the star, and the larger stars end their lives as explosive supernovas, thereby redistributing much of the chemically altered matter around the universe. According to the standard picture, the carbon and oxygen so essential to our own lives was produced in exactly this way.

From this remark alone it is clear that the precise nature of the matter contained in the universe is an important factor in determining its future. There are a number of effects that can change this material content. One is simply the expansion of the universe: as the universe expands, its constituents are cooled, and therefore – since the properties and composition of matter depend on temperature – the internal structure of the universe changes as time evolves.

There is also the question of the fundamental stability of matter. It is quite possible that there are extremely slow physical processes by which protons and neutrons will ultimately be converted into pure radiation, thereby destroying every atom and molecule in the universe. This is certainly a prediction of the more believable of the 'grand unified theories' that aspire to treat all atomic and nuclear forces as different facets of a single underlying force. However, no such events have been observed so far, and current limits on these processes mean that the era of 'proton decay' is at least 10^{32} years in the future.[8] In general, there might be other very slow processes (perhaps not as disastrous as proton decay) that have not yet been observed, but that could be very important in the later stages of the universe. Or there might be novel processes whose very possibility will only be conceivable to us at some unforeseen time in the future: a painful thought, perhaps, for scientific sensibility, but certainly not a logical impossibility; indeed, scientists do give serious consideration to speculations of this type.

Of even greater significance than the detailed constituents of matter is the force of gravity that pulls any two objects towards each other. For everyday things – like this page – the electrical repulsion between the positive nuclei in an atom and the negative orbiting electrons is much stronger than the attractive gravitational force, and a complete 'gravitational collapse' cannot occur. However, the force of gravity has the fundamental property that for any given material – be it paper or the intergalactic medium – when a large enough sample is considered, gravity will overwhelm all other forces. Thus, for objects that are larger than a critical size (the so called 'Jeans radius', which depends on the type of matter), gravitational collapse is inevitable.[9]

In practice, the victory of gravity may be Pyrrhic, since the system typically heats as it collapses, and this may change the properties of the matter until a new balance is reached. However, for objects with a sufficiently high density, gravity overcomes all resistance through the formation of black holes from which nothing can escape, except via very weak quantum processes (the famous 'Hawking radiation').

The Jeans collapse can also be avoided by an expanding universe in which more distant objects recede faster than nearby ones, and this may be sufficient to counteract the force of gravity. In effect, there is a size-dependent Jeans length that can prevent gravity from ever winning.

In a homogeneous expanding universe such as ours, whether or not gravity will eventually win depends on how much matter is present. In particular, given the current, empirical expansion rate, the critical mass density of our universe is computed to be approximately 4×10^{-30} grams per cubic centimetre. In a homogeneous model, if the mass density is above this critical value the universe is said to be 'closed', and it will eventually collapse under its own weight, with everything being crushed into an infinitesimally small region with infinite density. Although this collapse process would look quite similar to a time-reversed Big Bang, there is no scientific reason to expect the thermodynamic or psychological arrows of time to reverse as the universe re-collapses; in particular, any such collapse is expected to lie in our psychological future.

Observations have not yet determined definitely whether the universe is above or below the critical density. The most visible matter is in the form of stars, and the density in stars adds up to only around 1–2% of the critical value. One can also infer the presence of 'dark matter' by observing the effects of its gravitational pull on luminous objects,[10] as in the phenomenon of 'gravitational lensing', in which diverging light rays from an object can be refocussed by a large piece of (possibly unseen) matter to produce a characteristic visual image that includes more than one copy of the object. From such arguments, a convincing case can be made for a dark-matter density of around 10% of critical value, and there is also a weaker case for a total density that is quite close to the critical value. This is an area that is expected to become much clearer in the next five to ten years.

Another key issue concerning the future of the cosmos is that the current cosmological theories predict the existence of vast tracts of universe that have not yet been observed, in the fundamental sense that there has not been enough time since the Big Bang for light from these regions to reach us. More precisely, the observed universe has been around for about 10 billion years and therefore – because nothing can travel faster than light – the most distant objects we can observe are around 10 billion light-years[11] away. What lies beyond this horizon? In another 10 billion years the radius of the observed universe will have doubled, and this much larger observable region will then be able to affect the future of our cosmic corner. Anything said by a scientist about this as yet unobserved domain is inevitably highly speculative. In particular – and not withstanding the impressive sounding name of 'the Cosmological Principle' – this applies to the postulate that the entire universe, including the unobserved regions, is homogeneous. A set of popular theoretical ideas, called the 'Inflationary Universe', currently offer our best (albeit still incomplete) way of understanding the initial conditions for the Big-Bang. In an inflationary cosmology, matter enters a phase in which ordinary Einstein gravity becomes repulsive, thereby 'inflating' the growth of the universe by an enormous factor. Most inflationary models predict a region of homogeneity that reaches far beyond the current horizon, but even in these models the homogeneity does not extend for ever.

Thus current speculation prefers the – rather unexciting – view that what we shall see in another ten billion years, or even another billion billion years, is simply more of the same. However, there are numerous other possibilities. Just hidden from view there could be a shell of matter careering down on us that will eventually crush our part of the universe into a black hole; as far as we are concerned, this would lead to essentially the same scenario as that of a closed universe. It is also possible that, just hidden from view, there is a boundary beyond which lies a completely different form of matter; perhaps even occupying a different number of spatial dimensions, as is possible, for example, within the context of superstring theory – one of the most popular current contenders for unifying general relativity and quantum physics. Such a boundary might be the source of all kinds of exotic radiation that could destroy the world as we know it.

It is certainly possible that one of these radical possibilities could emerge during the current epoch – that is, over the next several billion years. Even in the inflationary picture – in which much larger regions of homogeneity are expected – there is still the question of what lies *outside* the homogeneous domain; in particular, it is quite possible that – even if the inflationary picture is correct – any one of the above events could eventually take place, albeit in an amount of time that makes 10 billion years look like a passing moment.

III. A standard scenario for the future of the universe

The long-term future of the universe involves a detailed interplay between the factors identified above, and – to re-emphasize our earlier caution – the extreme relevance of the unobserved region means that any attempt to predict such a future is necessarily highly speculative. However, we shall now sketch what might be expected within a 'standard' scenario in which it is assumed, optimistically, that the universe outside the currently observed region is very similar to what is seen within it.[12]

As a preliminary caveat we remark that, in order for a physical question to be well defined, it is often crucial to specify precisely who, or what, the 'observer' is: famously, this is one of the key ingredients in the theory of relativity; more subtly, it also plays a central role in the interpretation of quantum theory. When contemplating the end of the universe, the matter of choosing an observer can be a tricky one. The perspective of an individual who falls into a black hole will be completely different from that of someone who is sitting in a more ordinary corner of the universe. For the most part we shall avoid this particular problem by restricting our attention to the future evolution of the matter we can currently observe in the universe. It turns out that a great deal of a concrete nature can be said about this without needing to introduce the complexity of contextualizing the predictions to a particular observational framework.

The first significant change on the cosmic scale is expected in around 10^{14} years, when the stars will stop forming and the old stars will die out. This stems from continuous changes in the chemical composition of the universe due to stellar burning that will eventually result in a chemical composition which cannot be used as stellar fuel. Once all the stars are dead, the universe will be left with various stellar remnants: 'brown dwarfs', 'white dwarfs', 'neutron stars', and even black holes. Some of these will continue to emit light for a few billion years, but eventually they will all become very cold objects, since they lack the nuclear fuel necessary to remain luminous. On very rare occasions these objects could collide, leading to further releases of energy and, in some cases, new stars. Larger objects should also be able to ignite different nuclear processes that will survive for a while.

The next relevant structure in the cosmic scale are the galaxies, which will remain collections of cold stellar remnants for some time to come. Via random gravitational interactions, some stellar remnants will gain enough energy to break away from the containing galaxy, leaving the lower-energy remnants to fall towards the galactic centre, where they will form a black hole. In about 10^{19} years, most of the remnants will have broken free, leaving a central black hole with 1%–10% of the mass of the original galaxy. Galaxies are known to contain matter that is not in the form of stars (the so-called 'dark matter'), and a popular idea is that this dark matter is in the form of 'WIMPs' (Weakly Interacting Massive Particles) spread throughout the galaxy. These would annihilate into radiation in around 10^{23}–10^{25} years.

It is expected that at some point between 10^{32} and 10^{170} years from now, the protons and neutrons will decay into radiation. This will destroy the stellar remnants in the form of brown or white dwarfs, but not the black holes. However, black holes can decay through quantum effects to produce Hawking radiation, and all the black holes are expected to have vanished in this way in around 10^{100} years from now.

After the demise of the black holes, all the interesting features we know in the universe will have been erased, leaving nothing but extremely low-energy radiation. The only significant developments thereafter will be determined by whatever new features, if any, that enter into the ever-growing observable domain. Any viable model is expected to predict some chance that an over-dense region will appear and form a black hole; any such black holes will then eventually decay by the process mentioned above.

It is interesting to note that this reliable (albeit extremely rare) collapse of radiation into a black hole – whose energy is then randomly re-radiated during the decay – strongly reflects the steady evolution from simple to complex that lies behind the thermodynamic arrow of time. Thus one interesting feature of the known universe – the thermodynamic arrow of time – *does* remain. Some scientists view this arrow as the most essential ingredient of life, and even speculate that as long as there is such an arrow, new 'exotic' life forms could still emerge (and, presumably, reflect anxiously on whatever future of the universe still remains).

Note, however, that the persistence in this scenario of the thermo-dynamic arrow of time is really nothing more than a direct consequence of our starting premises. In particular, the assumption that the universe outside the observed domain is similar to what is currently seen may seem a modest one but, when one contemplates all the different states of matter that are possible, it becomes clear that the supposition of such a homogeneous starting point imposes a rigid *prima facie* simplicity on the early universe. The persistence of the thermodynamic arrow of time can then be traced to the steady degrading of this assumed initial simplicity as the universe evolves into a more complex state.

In the end, the further one tries to extrapolate our understanding of the universe, the more it depends on things we do not yet know. The honest appraisal of the scientific situation is that, ultimately, we will just have to wait and see what happens.

Notes

1. For example, see C. J. Isham, 'Creation of the universe as a quantum tunnelling process', in *Our Knowledge of God and Nature: Physics, Philosophy and Theology*, ed. R. J. Russell, W. Stoeger and G. Coyne, Notre Dame 1988, 374–408.

2. For a lively attack on such writings see Mary Midgley, *Science as Salvation*, London 1992.

3. A 'billion' is one thousand million.

4. In this context we might recall the famous philosophical discussion of 'grue', a colour that is green up to a certain time and blue thereafter.

5. Strictly speaking, these are not exact solutions, since the mathematics breaks down with a singularity at the beginning and end of each 'cycle'.

6. The only exception is a rather exotic decay process for K-mesons.

7. Optimists may wish to note that increased solar winds during this period could possibly push the earth into a larger orbit at a safe distance from the sun.

8. We use scientific notation in which, for example, $10^{14} = 100,000,000,000,000$ (the 14 counts the number of zeros after the '1'). One billion is 10^9.

9. For star-forming regions in the universe, the Jeans radius of the intergalactic material is approximately 10^{16}m.

10. Some authors have suggested that modifications to the laws of gravity rather than the presence of dark matter could also explain these observations, but a convincing model which explains all the observations has yet to emerge.

11. A 'light-year' is the distance travelled by light in a year.

12. An excellent recent review article is Fred C. Adams and Gregory Laughlin, 'A Dying Universe', *Reviews of Modern Physics*, 1997, 337–72.

IV · Expecting the End

The Appeal of the Apocalyptic

Stephen D. O'Leary

'Watchman, what time of night?
Watchman, what time of night?'
The watchman answers,
'Morning is coming, then night again'
(Isaiah 21.11–12, Jerusalem Bible)

As we approach the year 2000, the evidence of an upsurge of apocalypticism is overwhelming. In certain Catholic circles, interest in the purported prophecies of Garabandal and Fatima waxes strong, while reports abound of the Virgin Mary's miraculous apparitions from Medjugorge to Conyers, Georgia. In the Protestant world, fundamentalist and evangelical churches (often adhering to a dispensationalist theology of the End Times) are gaining in strength, while charismatic outpourings such as the 'Toronto Blessing' are seen by many as a miraculous manifestation of God's Spirit in the last days. Outside (and occasionally within) the Christian churches, millions of devotees of the so-called 'New Age' movement blend an eclectic mix of health fads, aboriginal spirituality, UFOs, prophecy and occultism into idiosyncratic new religions, whose only evident common feature is a pronounced resistance to traditional spiritual authority. Like roosters crowing the coming dawn, prophets of doomsday or of a bright millennial future appear in many colourful guises; their clamouring cries of imminent catastrophe and redemption – whether ecological, spiritual, economic or political in nature – vie for attention in the human barnyard. Today's watchmen, those who find themselves in positions of social and pastoral authority as we navigate the transition from the last days of the passing millennium to the first years of the new, would do well to study these cries and note how and to whom they appeal. For heedless crowing can confuse and scatter the flocks, making them easy prey for the foxes and wolves, the false messiahs who abound in our benighted culture. The recent ritual suicides of the Solar Temple and Heaven's Gate cults in France, Switzerland, Canada and the United States; the poison gas attacks in the subways of Tokyo sponsored by the apocalyptic Aum Shinrikyo; and other events in our news headlines, make the lesson clear: millennial beliefs are fraught with serious consequences, and require careful examination and understanding.

A comprehensive account of the historical, sociological and psychological origins of apocalypticism is hardly possible here. I am charged with brevity, and in any case one would be hard pressed to locate a consensus among the variety of disparate explanations for apocalyptic phenomena offered by social scientists. My modest purpose here is to review and critique briefly the social-science literature on apocalyptic movements, and to suggest that these lead naturally to a conception of apocalyptic as a symbolic theodicy, a mythological solution to the problem of evil, pain and suffering. I then briefly consider the role of new forms of mass-mediated communication in fomenting and sustaining the contemporary apocalyptic mood. Finally, I conclude with an appeal for a mode of millennial understanding that takes the appeal of apocalypse seriously without over-dramatizing our own historical moment.

How are we to understand the enduring appeal of apocalypticism, in spite of the repeated disappointments suffered by believers through the centuries? Any answer to this question must begin with a cohesive definition of the phenomenon itself. Norman Cohn's classic study *The Pursuit of the Millennium* provides an influential formulation adequate for this discussion. Cohn defines the type of salvation that is the object of the millennial movement's expectation as *collective, terrestrial, imminent, total and miraculous* (Cohn, 13). This definition of millennial aspirations can encompass a variety of phenomena, from mediaeval or modern Christian movements, through the 'Ghost Dance' religion of the Plains Indians in the nineteenth century, to the famous 'cargo cults' of Melanesia. However, when we attempt to move beyond common features of millennial hopes across cultures to comparison of the historical and social contexts in which versions of these hopes arose, the problem becomes more difficult. In attempting to answer the question of *why* a movement (or occasionally, a whole society) has expressed its aspirations in this particular form, social scientists have naturally explored the conditions that have given birth to millennialism, seeking common features or experiences among a wide variety of groups and social contexts in order to define the factors that condition audiences for millennial discourse to an acceptance of its claims. Thus, for example,

Frank Kermode speaks of an 'apocalyptic set – a state of affairs in which one can discern some sociological predisposition to the acceptance of apocalyptic structures and figures' (Kermode 1985, 86).

The factors that are said to define this 'apocalyptic set' vary widely. One group of scholars views millennial cults in essentially economic political terms, as 'The Religions of the Oppressed' (Lanternari). The various incarnations of apocalyptic belief are seen as responses by dispossessed workers and minorities to conditions of industrial and colonial oppression, material deprivation, and the social dislocations of modernity. The audience for apocalyptic discourse is thus defined in terms of its material class and conditions. Thus Hobsbawm describes certain European apocalyptic groups as 'Primitive Rebels', composed of 'small struggling peasants, agricultural craftsmen, village artisans, and the like' (Hobsbawm, 71), while Worsley argues that millennarian beliefs primarily comprise a 'religion of the lower orders', which remains perennially appealing in spite of disappointment 'precisely because they make such a strong appeal to the oppressed, the disinherited and the wretched' (Worsley, 225). In similar terms, as Cohn attempts to account for both primitive and modern millennial movements, he argues that modern apocalyptic groups are composed of 'certain politically marginal elements in technologically advanced societies – chiefly young or unemployed workers and a small minority of intellectuals and students' (Cohn 1970, 285–6).

The characterization of apocalyptic enthusiasts as victims of colonial oppression or economic marginalization may be adequate for native cargo cults or for millennial movements in peasant societies making the difficult transition from agricultural to industrial economies: they are clearly not helpful for understanding much of contemporary millennialism. To choose but one example, the American author Hal Lindsey is among the best-selling authors of the closing decades of the twentieth century; the tens of millions of middle-class Americans who have purchased his *The Late Great Planet Earth* can hardly be numbered among the wretched of the earth. Nor can they truthfully be labelled as 'politically marginal' in a country where a substantial fundamentalist Christian constituency has had a profound impact on both local and national politics. In fact, a brief glance at the history of apocalyptic discourse shows that its appeal has historically cut across class lines. The audience of those receptive to prophecy and its interpreters has included kings, emperors, peasants and presidents, merchants, farmers and factory workers, the educated and the uneducated alike, from Isaac Newton to Ronald Reagan. Mechanistic theories of apocalyptic as a response to economic circumstance fail to account for this wide variety of class and education in apocalyptic audiences.

An objective experience of oppression or economic deprivation is clearly not a necessary precondition for the flourishing of millennial beliefs. The theory of relative deprivation offered by some sociologists is somewhat more sophisticated in that it seeks to account for the role of perception in predisposing audiences to apocalyptic conversion. David Aberle defines relative deprivation as 'a negative discrepancy between legitimate expectation and actuality' (Aberle, 209); seeking to ground the theory in measurable factors, he classifies the relative experience of deprivation into categories of possessions, status, behaviour and worth, and argues that deprivation in one or more of these areas may result in adherence to apocalyptic belief. This explanation has certain advantages, in that it does help us to understand how persons or groups who enjoy a comfortable existence may become susceptible to millennial beliefs when they compare their situation to others who are better off. However, while possessions, status, behaviour and worth may be quantifiable in some sense, it is much harder to measure the subjective experience of lack that comes from a comparison of one's own social position and goods to those of others. Regarding the relative deprivation model, A. Y. Collins comments that 'The crucial element is not so much whether one is actually oppressed as whether one feels oppressed' (Collins, 84). This points out a primary difficulty which makes the concept of relative deprivation, however useful in the abstract, difficult to apply in specific cases. Subjective feelings of deprivation and oppression are not easy to measure, nor can they always be documented in millennial movements where members have often left little record of their interior experience.

An alternative explanation for the appeal of apocalyptic is offered by the political scientist and social historian Michael Barkun. His *Disaster and the Millennium* attempts to document the thesis that the main predisposing factor determining the apocalyptic set is the common experience of natural and man-made calamities. Barkun analyses apocalyptic movements in many cultures and historical eras, compiling much evidence to support his claim that 'disasters serve to predispose individuals to millenarian conversion'. His argument is weakened, however, by his own admissions that disaster 'is to some extent in the eye of the beholder', and that 'if the world has no disaster to offer, then one must be constructed' (Barkun 1974, 128, 60, 208). Clearly, these observations undercut the force of Barkun's thesis: for even if we allow that events such as earthquakes, wars and depressions are experienced as disasters by virtually everyone, not every event of this kind is accompanied by an increase in apocalyptic conversion, while events that are not clearly disastrous in any objective sense may take on the appearance of catastrophe when interpreted by audiences already predisposed to a millennial world view. We are thus confronted again with the difficulty of measuring intangible perceptions and subjective responses to events which take on different meanings that depend upon the interpretative framework through which they are perceived.

Barkun's subsequent study *Crucible of the Millennium* recognizes the problem with his earlier formulation of disaster as the dominant factor predisposing audiences towards millennial beliefs. Here he goes so far as to suggest that ' "disaster" functions as a mental construct which can be linked not only to observable death and destruction but to events that symbolize loss of control and meaning' (Barkun 1986, 153-4). This is typical of what we may call the 'anomic' theory of apocalypticism, which broadens the issue beyond the realms of economics and politics by including explicit considerations of psychology. Millennial believers are typically diagnosed by adherents of this school as prone to psychological conditions of 'anomie' and 'absence of meaning'. Thus, Barry Brummett contends that 'apocalyptic has a "hard-core" audience that suffers from an unusually strong sense of anomie or disorientation' (Brummett, 59). This sort of psychology may result from a collective experience of trauma or catastrophe, as Lifton shows. However, this diagnosis is subject to the same problems and limitations as the relative deprivation concept, in that traumatic experiences are just as often rooted in the perceptual realm. Brummett adds that the 'anomic audience is motivated by the perception of disasters which cannot be explained by received systems of meaning' (Brummett, 59). This conception is clearly relevant to our inquiry, but it complicates the question considerably. The early Christians who responded favourably to the book of Revelation were, by most historical accounts, subject to intense persecution that included execution and public torture. If the largely middle-class group of fundamentalist Christians in the United States who today form the core of Hal Lindsey's readership believes itself to be similarly persecuted, this is surely a rhetorically induced perception; for there is an obvious difference between being torn apart by lions in front of cheering crowds and being forced to endure media onslaughts of sex, violence and secular humanism. The problem of perception thus appears to be insurmountable: while clinicians may objectively diagnose a condition of anomie or disorientation, the root causes of these internal states are not to be found in objective events, but in the perceived inability of existing systems of meaning to account for the vicissitudes of historical fortune and everyday life.

Among the more noteworthy attempts to apply a psychological model to the explanation of millennialism is Cohn's discussion of apocalyptic fantasies as a 'paranoid' response to economic deprivation and political persecution. In the original edition of his *Pursuit of the Millennium*, Cohn argues that those who seek an adequate explanation of millennial movements

> cannot afford to ignore the psychic content of the phantasies which have inspired them. All these phantasies are precisely such as are commonly found in individual cases of paranoia. The megalomaniac view of oneself as the elect, wholly good, abominably persecuted, yet assured of ultimate triumph; the attribution of gigantic and demonic powers to the adversary; the refusal to accept the ineluctable limitations and imperfections of human existence, such as transience, dissension, conflict, fallibility, whether intellectual or moral; the obsession with inerrable prophecies – these attitudes are symptoms which together constitute the unmistakable syndrome of paranoia. But a paranoiac delusion does not cease to be so because it is shared by so many individuals, nor yet because those individuals have real and ample grounds for regarding themselves as victims of oppression (Cohn 1957, 309).

While I find this interpretation quite persuasive, so far as it goes, we should be exceedingly cautious in applying modern psychological concepts to patients long dead, or beyond the reach of clinical study. One must pause at the implications of considering millennial apocalypticism as a disease of the mind, or as a symptom of such disorders. What is gained by such understanding is, perhaps, a degree of insight into the mind-set of historical and contemporary groups; but the prevalence of this pathology in a variety of canonical scriptures may lead to some uncomfortable lines of questioning. Further, even if the diagnosis is accepted, we have not solved the question of origins; when millennialism is understood as a version of paranoia, or as a symptom of such a psychic affliction, the aetiology of this strange affliction is still unexplained, and we have yet to account for the peculiar forms that it takes. Finally, psychological explanations suffer from the same defect as theories based on causal factors such as oppression and injustice: namely, that such factors are unfortunately omnipresent throughout history. The prevalence of psychic conditions such as anxiety, apprehension, dissatisfaction and even paranoia leads me to wonder, not why we become apocalyptic, but why any of us are not apocalyptic, or whether we are not all incipient millennialists.

No survey of social-scientific approaches to the phenomenon of apocalyptic belief would be complete without mentioning Leon Festinger's influential theory of cognitive dissonance. Since the publication of the classic *When Prophecy Fails: A Social and Psychological Study of a Modern Group that Predicted the Destruction of the World*, Festinger's theory has become a standard part of the description of the dynamics of apocalyptic sects and movements. The term 'cognitive dissonance' refers to a mental state of discomfort created by any undeniable event (or non-event) that contradicts a deeply-held belief – such as the failure of Christ to return to a predicted date. The assumption is that human beings are motivated to reduce or eliminate such discomfort by whatever means possible. Festinger and his co-authors predicted that, in certain circumstances (when predictions are specific enough, when believers have sufficiently committed themselves, and when the proper forms of social support are present), the disconfirmation of a deeply held belief may result in increased proselytizing and a strengthening, rather than abandonment, of the belief system. Practically speaking, this seems nothing more than an example of the logical fallacy known as the 'bandwagon effect', which holds that 'if more and more people can be persuaded that the system of belief is correct, then clearly, it must, after all, be correct' (Festinger et al., 18).

Seeking a test of their theory, Festinger and his colleagues lighted upon a local UFO cult that predicted the arrival of flying saucers and the rescue of a faithful core of believers on a certain date in 1951. They infiltrated the group in order to study the mental processes of rationalization that accompanied the non-appearance of the predicted space ships. The case study lent qualified support to the theory, but the evidence from other studies of the phenomenon which attempt to replicate Festinger's finding appears to be inconclusive. Not all groups which experience prophetic failure increase their proselytizing in the aftermath: some may abandon the belief-system, while others may choose different means to reduce dissonance, such as reinterpreting the prophecy or minimizing contact with non-believers. Since Festinger's theory could have predicted any of these consequences, it seems to be circular. That is to say, the existence of a mental condition is used to explain behaviour, but the same behaviour constitutes our only evidence for the existence of the condition. While this constitutes a serious flaw in Festinger's theory, it does not detract from the descriptive utility of the dissonance concept, nor has it prevented scholars from applying the concept to the study of apocalyptic sects, and even to the early history of the Christian church itself. Most notably, John Gager's *Kingdom and Community* employs dissonance theory in an analysis of 'Earliest Christianity as a millennial movement' (Gager, 20), regarding the fact of the crucifixion as the original 'dissonance event' which appeared to contradict the messianic prophecies of Israel's restored kingdom.

Thus, all simplistic causal explanations for this phenomenon – whether based on external, natural, economic or political causes, or on internal, emotional and psychological causes – can be shown to have failed. Howard Kaminsky exposes the inherent circularity of such attempts: 'If we bear in mind the kind of causative factors that [scholars have considered for millennial movements] – anxiety, sense of deprivation, social suffering, etc. – we must admit that in no single case is it even remotely possible to deduce the movement from any single factor, any group of factors, or any definable degree of intensity of such factors. All such efforts lead directly to the circle: X is alleged to be necessary for the movement, but the only way we know that X is present is that the movement has come into being' (Kaminsky, 216).

Given this circularity, it may be more fruitful to think of apocalypticism not as a series of *movements* with discrete and identifiable causes in historical events, but rather as a *tradition*, a textually embodied community of discourse founded in the accepted canon of Western sacred texts and occasionally augmented by the production of new revelations and interpretative strategies. This complicates the problem of explaining the appeal of apocalyptic discourse. We are confronted with a continuous textual tradition, maintained and embroidered by a discourse of exegesis and commentary fostered in learned and elite circles, which at various historical intervals has erupted into more mainstream popular discourse through movements inspired sometimes by new prophecies and sometimes by new interpretations of canonical texts. Apocalyptic rhetoric has always found audiences, though the size and composition of these audiences have varied greatly over the centuries. No simple explanations will account for the increased popularity of apocalypticism that historians have documented in mediaeval Europe, in Renaissance England, or in the United States during the early nineteenth and late twentieth centuries. Likewise, no theory has been proposed that successfully accounts for the extreme varieties of behaviour exhibited by those who expect the End in their lifetimes, from fervent proselytizing to passive withdrawal from the world, from revolutionary terrorism to quiet pacifism, from extreme celibacy (even to the point of repeating the self-mutilation of Origen) to the most profligate forms of antinomian sexuality (including promiscuity and polygamy).

Deprivation, oppression, anomie, disaster, dissonance – what are these theories but partial explanations, glimpses and fragments of a truth seen through a glass darkly, which each point in their own way to a deeper truth not only about apocalypticism but about the human condition itself? Apocalyptic was accepted into the canon of scripture, and maintains a vital presence in most if not all of the world's faith traditions, because the problem that it grapples with is precisely the fundamental problem of religion: theodicy, or the necessity of providing a coherent assertion of meaning in the face of death and suffering. For those whose fear of death becomes an obsession, apocalypse offers the chance to forget our own mortality by projecting our fears on to a cosmic screen, imagining an all-engulfing catastrophe that is to be welcomed rather than feared. Suffering is not experienced only by the downtrodden: to be born human is to be deprived. We are all oppressed, if not by other humans then by our very human limitations: anomie is an ever-present possibility; the world never lacks for natural and symbolic disasters, whether these are experienced personally or vicariously. The real cognitive dissonance (to which any thinking moral person is subject) is an intense and entirely praiseworthy discomfort that comes from acknowledging the gap between the world as it is and the world as it should be. Though visions of a perfected society may differ, our depictions of a restored pastoral garden or of the Heavenly City perform an indispensable function. While we confront the catastrophes of history, they allow us to maintain what the Marxist historian Ernst Bloch calls 'the principle of hope' – the faith in a *telos*, an end, a goal towards which we are moving, in which all injustices will be righted and all mysteries unveiled.

We cannot end our enquiry here, however, for there is one novel aspect of contemporary apocalypticism which deserves discussion. I refer to the astonishing growth of electronic media in the twentieth century. In his book *Century's End*, Hillel Schwartz characterizes millennial consciousness as 'a sense of omnipresent, accelerating change [accompanied by] a widespread notion that this is the ultimate, critical moment, and that we are on the "event horizon"' (Schwartz, 243). While the sense of change accelerating to a critical moment of crisis has been experienced by believers going back to the earliest Christians and before them, I would submit that the media magnifies this age-old sensibility to an unprecedented degree. The advent of modern communication technologies has fundamentally altered the cultural and social situation for apocalyptic discourse by 1. increasing both the amount and the types of information available for millennialists to construct their webs of meaning; 2. standardizing calendar and clock time, and habituating us to measuring time in smaller and smaller units, thereby increasing our awareness of time's passage; 3. making possible the formation of new types of communities united not by geography but by shared interests and access to electronic media – so that we now witness millennial cults forming on computer networks, and recruiting on the World Wide Web.

Consider two of the traditional signs supposed to accompany the apocalypse: 'wars and rumours of wars' and earthquakes. Human nature being what it is, there have always been ongoing conflicts taking place around the globe at any one point in time. But now we have CNN to be there with the television cameras, and images of death and destruction appear in everyone's living room, Internet users may log on and be treated to live or nearly instantaneous personal reports of such events as a coup in Russia, or bombing attacks in Israel. Likewise, in the natural flow of geological time, we see that earthquakes have always been a daily occurrence around the world and that their frequency may ebb and flow according to natural processes, such as plate tectonics, which we dimly understand. But major tremors that once would have gone unreported, or about which we might previously not have learned for months, if not years, are now reported on the nightly news; and geological data from around the world are now posted to Internet sites and monitored carefully by millennialists anticipating both geological catastrophes (known as 'Earth Changes' in New Age circles) and the return of Jesus.

The unique capability of electronic media users simultaneously to monitor multiple events and processes in the global theatre creates a new awareness of time and of the weight of historical action. This experience of time and the associated expectation of a moment of singularity is sharply manifested in the contemporary apocalyptic mood; and the media is clearly an active force in shaping, and not merely transmitting, apocalypticism. A case in point can be found in the notorious 'Heaven's Gate' suicide cult. This group gives a new and terrifying significance to popular media products which had long enjoyed what are commonly, and unthinkingly, referred to as 'cult followings': the 'X-files', 'Star Trek', and 'Star Wars'. The importance of film and television in the group's belief system is evident from the video suicide notes they left behind, which contain repeated references to science-fiction scenarios. Most strikingly, the following self-description from the group's Web page, with which they sought to explain and justify their mission, puts the role of the popular media into sharp relief: 'To help you understand who we are, we have taken the liberty to express a brief synopsis in the vernacular of a popular "science fiction" entertainment series. Most readers in the late twentieth century will certainly recognize the intended parallels. It is really quite interesting to see how the context of fiction can often open the mind to advanced possibilities which are, in reality, quite close to fact.' The document continues with a theme familiar to science-fiction buffs worldwide: 'Extraterrestrials Return with Final Warning'.

The members of Heaven's Gate were surely deluded about the existence of alien rescuers and the redemptive value of suicide, but their insight into popular culture is both accurate and profound. The media play a significant role in the social acceptance and growing plausibility of apocalyptic beliefs and millennial scenarios. There is ample evidence that the willing suspension of disbelief demanded in our narrative fictions and our tabloid press now extends to religion and politics in new and distressing ways, and that this effect is not confined to suicidal cultists. Conspiracy theories which were once relegated to the fringe of politics in the United States are now increasingly plausible among the mainstream of our citizenry: approximately half of the USA believes in the reality of alien visitors and the cover-up of extra-terrestrial presences by the government. Even for the sober-minded, who are less prone to confuse fiction and fact, the saturation of media coverage that will accompany the transition into the third millennium is bound to raise expectations. As never before, there will be a global awareness of the passage of a single moment of time which will focus attention on hopes and fears for the future.

As we witness the parade of millennial foolishness that the next few years will bring, we would do well to remember the words of St Augustine, whose own crisis-filled time offers instructive parallels to our own. Augustine reminds us that empires may crumble, but hope springs eternal. He cautioned those who saw evidences of impending apocalypse in the fifth century to remember that the signs of the end are always present:

Certainly, the Apostle [Paul] said . . . that in the last days shall come on savage times . . . and describes what they will be like, saying 'Men shall be lovers of themselves, lovers of money, haughty, proud, blasphemous, disobedient to parents, ungrateful, wicked, irreligious, without affection, slanderers, incontinent, unmerciful, without kindness, traitors, stubborn, blind, lovers of pleasures more than of God, having an appearance of godliness but denying the power thereof.' I wonder if such men have ever been lacking . . . As to wars, when has not the earth been scourged by them at different periods and places?

Augustine warns us against the excesses of apocalyptic excitement, urging a sceptical view of the claims of millennialists so that 'when we fall into a panic over present happenings as if they were the ultimate and extreme of all things, we may not be laughed at by those who have read more and worse things in the history of the world' (Augustine, 384, 387). His is a message that pastors around the world will need to articulate forcefully in the years ahead.

Bibliography

D. F. Aberle, 'A Note on Relative Deprivation Theory as applied to Millenarian and Other Cult Movements', in *Millennial Dreams in Action: Studies in Revolutionary Religious Movements*, ed. Sylvia Thrupp, New York 1970, 209–14.

Augustine, 'To Hesychius. On the End of the World' (Letter 99), in *Writings of Saint Augustine*, Vol. 12, trans. Sister Wilfrid Parsons, New York 1955, 356–401.

M. Barkun, *Disaster and the Millennium*, New Haven 1974.

——, *Crucible of the Millennium*, Syracuse, NY 1986.

E. Bloch, *The Principle of Hope*, Oxford and Cambridge, Mass. 1986.

B. Brummett, 'Using Apocalyptic Discourse to Exploit Audience Commitments through "Transfer" ', *Southern Speech Communication Journal* 54, 1988, 58–73.

K. Burridge, *New Heaven, New Earth: A Study of Millenarian Activities*, Oxford 1969.

N. Cohn, *In Pursuit of the Millennium*, London 1957 (revised ed. London 1980).

A. Y. Collins, *Crisis and Catharsis: The Power of the Apocalypse*, Philadelphia 1954.

L. Festinger, H. Riecken and S. Schachter, *When Prophecy Fails: A Social and Psychological Study of a Modern Group that Predicted the Destruction of the World*, New York 1964.

J. Gager, *Kingdom and Community: The Social World of Early Christianity*, Englewood Cliffs, NJ 1975.

E. J. Hobsbawm, *Primitive Rebels, Studies in Archaic Forms of Social Movements in the Nineteenth and Twentieth Centuries*, New York 1959.

H. Kaminsky, 'The Problem of Explanation', in *Millennial Dreams in Action: Studies in Revolutionary Religious Movements*, ed. Sylvia Thrupp, New York 1970.

F. Kermode, 'Apocalypse and the Modern', in *Visions of Apocalypse: End or Rebirth?*, ed. Saul Friedlander, Gerald Horton, Leo Marx and Eugene Skolnikoff, New York 1985.

V. Lanternari, *The Religions of the Oppressed: A Study of Modern Messianic Cults*, New York 1985.

R. J. Lifton, 'The Image of the End of the World: A Psychohistorical View', in

Visions of Apocalypse: End or Rebirth?, ed. Saul Friedlander, Gerald Horton, Leo Marx and Eugene Skolnikoff, New York 1985.

H. Lindsey, *The Late Great Planet Earth*, New York 1970.

H. Schwartz, *Century's End: A Cultural History of the Fin de Siècle from the 990s through the 1990s*, New York 1990.

P. Worsley, *The Trumpet Shall Sound*, New York 1968.

The Birth Pains of the Kingdom of God

Apocalypses of the Poor in Latin America

Marcelo Barros

If one day you, reader, should visit Brazil in early October, I suggest you include the hinterland of Bahia in your itinerary. There you will find yourself caught up in a pilgrimage that every year brings together thousands of people from all classes and from all sorts of community organizations. From all regions of the country, the crowd assembles in a poor and distant village in the high scrubland of Bahia. The journey is hard, the climate one of the most inhospitable in the whole north-east of Brazil. Nature has been destroyed, the land is dry, and the virtually non-existent vegetation hardly invites anyone to stay in such a place. There is little to show that a hundred years ago a community of several thousand flourished: the place was called Canudos (canes) on account of the abundant bulrushes that grew on the banks of the river Vasa-barris. People say that at the time Canudos was the second city of the state of Bahia. By sharing with you here the experience of those brothers and sisters who gave their lives believing that the Lord was about to put the promise of his liberating coming into effect with them, I invite you to relate this experience to that of many Christian communities from the lower strata of society who live their faith and hope in the kingdom on the basis of reading the Apocalypse. I should like to recount their experience as though I were going with you on a pilgrimage to the world of the very poorest, to share in the pain and hope of those who suffer like the prophet John, 'your brother who shares with you in Jesus the persecution and the kingdom and the patient endurance' (Rev. 1.9).

I. An awkward memory

In October 1897 the Brazilian army massacred the community of Canudos. Their leader, Antônio Conselheiro, was a simple poor man. He practised as a lawyer and taught in the hinterland of Ceará. One day his wife left him, and he became a pilgrim. He travelled on foot all over the scrubland of north-eastern Brazil, from Ceará to Bahia, counselling poor people, building churches, cemeteries and dams and proclaiming the imminent coming of the Lord and his justice. He called the poor to come and live together, sharing their goods and waiting for the coming of the Lord.

Conselheiro knew the biblical prophets and the Apocalypse well. Basing himself on the Bible, he rescued landless peasants from their plight and farm workers from their wage slavery and welcomed escaped slaves into the community he established. He preached that the Republic just established in Brazil had no right to levy taxes on people who had already lost everything. 'If a power does not express the power of God in favour of justice, it is the power of the Beast and not of the Lamb. It is not legitimate and should not be obeyed.'

When government troops attacked Canudos, Conselheiro interpreted this as the fulfilment of the Apocalypse. The community of the servants of God was being attacked by two beasts: the government of the Republic and the hierarchy of the church. The community had the duty to resist. The workers would be the angels of God in the holy war that announced the final coming of Christ. Using cannons and other heavy weapons, the soldiers attacked and murdered everyone, including women and children. They cut the throats of prisoners, even if they were already dead. The houses were burned and the land later flooded, so that the memory of the massacre would be buried.

History books gave no account of this and the newspapers published nothing. But the people did not forget; in recent years they have revived the memory of Canudos. They pulled a large wooden cross from the waters, said to be the very cross that Conselheiro carried on his travels through the scrubland. This cross is carried by peasants continuing the struggle for land. Every year the people of the hinterland make a pilgrimage to the site of the massacre. There they remember their dead ancestors. For them, the memory of Canudos is not the story of a defeat but of a movement that, a hundred years later, is being reborn with the power of a hope that is God's promise.

II. 'Who here is from Philadelphia and who from Laodicea?' (Pentecostal apocalypses)

It was at a service of the Assembly of God, the largest Pentecostal church in Brazil, that I first heard this question asked by the pastor. The whole community joined in a song on the subject of the letters to the seven churches (Rev. 1.11). At the end, the pastor asked who belonged to the church of Philadelphia, the well-beloved: 'because you have kept my word of patient endurance, I will keep you from the hour of trial that is coming on the whole world to test the inhabitants of the earth' (Rev. 3.11, cf. 7–13). And who, on the other hand, belonged to the church of Laodicea, 'neither hot nor cold', a church that thought itself rich but was in fact 'wretched, pitiable, poor, blind, and naked' (3.15, 17, cf. 14–22). Of course, though some Catholic visitors did not know what to say, the Pentecostal community shouted out its adherence to the church of Philadelphia. Not one hand went up for Laodicea. For the most recent believers who still did not know the references, it was an ideal means of making them read the Apocalypse, linking it to the circumstances of their lives and their belonging to a particular church.

The very phenomenon of Pentecostalism has a lot to do with an apocalyptic interpretation of the Bible and of life itself. As we are drawing closer to these communities in a respectful pilgrimage, I shall not go into detailed or specialized classifications of them here. But some distinctions do need to be made. In Brazil, out of a population estimated at some 160,000,000, the number of evangelicals has risen to some 35,000,000, of whom about sixty per cent are Pentecostals.[1] The first Pentecostal churches arose in the United States early this century when Christians excluded from their churches of origin because they were black or immigrants[2] had an experience of the Spirit, found themselves preaching or speaking in tongues, formed autonomous groups, and came south to countries such as Brazil.[3] 'For the first Pentecostals, what authenticated divine intervention, besides miraculous cures and manifestations of the gift of tongues, was the abolition of social barriers.'[4]

Pentecostal churches seek God's intervention through baptism in the Spirit and the outpouring of its gifts. They read the Bible on the basis of this longing for the coming of the Lord. A pastor will often end a service by saying something like, 'Till next Sunday, if by then the Lord has not come to seize us up into the skies and take us with him away from this evil world.'

In Brazil the classical Pentecostal churches are the Assembly of God, the Christian Congregation of Brazil, the Church of Christ and the

Church of the Four Square Gospel, among others. From the 1960s onward other movements have arisen, forming a new type of Pentecostalism focussed not so much on the gifts of the Spirit and a reading of their faith on the basis of the Apocalypse as on the ministry of healing. They make great use of local radio and hold services to cast out demons and heal people. These churches, such as 'God is Love' and the 'House of Blessing', have, in turn, seen the rise of groups that have broken with them and founded other independent movements. These new churches, starting in the 1970s, are based on television programmes. Although they still keep Pentecostal elements, they are different from the churches of classical Pentecostalism. They may still speak of the Apocalypse and the coming of the Lord, but they are more syncretistic, taking some elements from popular Catholicism and others from the Pentecostal churches. They are involved in the world of politics and economic concerns. They make up what has generally become known as 'neo-Pentecostalism' or autonomous Pentecostalism.

They are in effect churches that make the continual reading of apocalyptic texts the main focus of their belief. For them, 'eschatology is the very key to understanding of the Christian faith'.[5] They read apocalyptic texts on the basis of popular culture. This is their way of protesting against the world, differentiating themselves from a clerical church linked to elites in society, and helping people to stand firm in the most difficult circumstances. This simple, popular reading of the Bible, even if it lacks a historical viewpoint, should not be seen as mere fundamentalism. The popular Pentecostal reading is different from fundamentalist reading because, though it may be ingenuous and ahistorical, it is not always dogmatic and reactionary. Research shows, for example, that most of the landless peasants in one of the areas where the land occupation movement is strongest (O Pontal de Paranapanema, in the state of Sao Paulo) are Pentecostals. Fundamentalism is fomented rather by (charismatic) Catholic and Protestant elites from a capitalist background, including groups that preach the 'theology of prosperity', such as Christian Science or the Full Gospel Businessmen's Society.

> Pentecostalism today is a great sign of the times, as the Reformation was in the sixteenth century, except that the Reformation started in alliance with the bourgeoisie [which was revolutionary at the time!] and the Pentecostal movement is linked to lower social strata, to the culture of the excluded.[6]

III. Messages to those in flight from the year 2000 (Apocalypses of groups excluded from the world and the churches)

Many people today have such a distorted view of reality that even businessmen and professional women are afraid of the year 2000 and produce detailed reasons for their fear. The rich are turning to private and ever more rationalist rituals, while the poorest have their own ways of expressing fear and their alternative strategems for fleeing from the dangers. Throughout Latin America, there is a proliferation of groups and movements using figures and images from apocalyptic texts as they await the end of the world at the end of the millennium. In Bolivia it is increasingly common to hear 'prophets' declaring, 'The world is coming to an end! At midnight on 31 December 1999 the angels will sound the trumpet and the world will be rolled up like a sheet.' The Aymara say that their prophets of old had foretold something similar. Many people are putting their trust in groups taking refuge in the sacred places of Lake Titicaca, or in Tiwahanacu, near the Gateway of the Sun.

All over Latin America prophets are announcing the end of time with increasing frequency and asking the poor people to give their labour free, not to mention money, to build houses in sacred places such as Machu Picchu and certain volcanoes in Central America, or on the shores of Lake Titicaca, in which the 'converted' can await the end of the world. By reconstructing Amazonian traditions or seeking out 'high energy' places, people are trying, perhaps unconsciously, to re-establish contact with age-old cultures in places like Bolivia, where many years ago, perhaps even two thousand years before Christ, the Tiwanaku civilization flourished, about which very little is known to date.[7] Such groups should be distinguished from organized churches and from Pentecostalism. They are fringe movements that mingle biblical apocalypse with their own indigenous traditions.

When we speak of apocalypses in Latin America, we usually think of the poorest groups in society, particularly Amerindians and those from Afro-American traditions. The poor have a special love of apocalyptic literature and read it 'from their sufferings and struggles'.[8] Generally speaking, images of the end of the world and the coming of the Lord frighten those who lead peaceful and secure lives in society. These same images inspire and strengthen persons and groups who are already suffering as much as or more than the afflictions described in the Apocalypse. On the peripheries of Latin American cities a family can go to sleep without knowing if its members will wake up alive or whether they will fall victim to the gangs that roam the *barrios*. A mother never knows if she will be the next in her alley to mourn the death of a child. Every day the poor go to work in insecurity and in fear of being sacked. In this context, the promises of the Apocalypse are liberating, even if, as in all wars, there is danger for everyone.

In the 1960s the Brazilian cinema sought to portray the immense social differences existing in Brazil and to show that two opposed worlds existed in the same country, but could not do so directly and openly because the military censorship prevented it. The ploy it devised was to speak of the present by portraying the past history of the scrubland with its 'blessed' and its 'gunmen', using an apocalyptic cast of language. Glauber Rocha made 'God and the Devil in the Land of the Sun' (or *Antônio das Mortes*), a film acclaimed at Cannes, and its successor, 'The Dragon of Evil against the Holy Warrior'. Both are interpretations of the actual state of affairs in Brazil seen through the traditions of popular religion. In them, people longing for God's intervention read the Apocalypse as applying directly to them, since they have nothing to hope for from their actual situation.

IV. Engaged communities and their apocalypses

I worked for fifteen years as theological adviser to the CPT (Pastoral Land Commission) and, with Carlos Mesters and others, was a member of the founding team of the CEBI (Ecumenical Bible Study Centre). Since 1978 I have been arranging Bible-study courses with peasants and people's groups in Brazil and Bolivia, as well as giving some courses in Nicaragua, Mexico and Cuba. In all these places, one of the subjects people ask for most often is a reading of the Apocalypse from their situation. They cite the same passages that Antônio Conselheiro used in his preaching a hundred years ago: the vision of the seven seals, the Woman who appears pregnant in the heavens, the Beast who comes from the sea, and the struggle of Babylon against the heavenly Jerusalem. They read the Bible on the basis of their harsh situation and they read life and its future with a hope given them by the Apocalypse.

Once in Itacatiara, in Amazonia, a base community leader explained the unrolling of the seven seals by counting the stages through which industrial ships had invaded their lakes and swamps and little by little, with industrial fishing equipment and huge refrigerators, had taken all the fish from the poor people who lived on the banks by fishing. This injustice left them gazing for a long time at the little fish floating dead on the now polluted waters that had been caught up in the nets and thrown back as of no interest to the commercial fishermen. Interpreting this story from the Apocalypse helped the community to organize the small fishermen to fight for their rights and to defend their waters.

I have preached three annual retreats for the pastoral agents of the prelacy of Sao Félix do Araguaia. The first was on the subject of the book of the Apocalypse and the message of hope that God gives through this book to a church witnessing to Christ the liberator in the midst of a situation of martyrdom. The other two times we closed the retreat by composing a sort of 'eighth letter of the Apocalypse' to the angel of the church of Sao Félix do Araguaia.

There is a profound difference between how the base church communities and Christians in other popular movements such as the Pentecostals, who have a presence in the encampments and settlements of landless peasants, read and interpret the Apocalypse and how groups and movements waiting for the end of the world do. The difference is that engaged communities enjoy the promises of the Apocalypse, feel stimulated by its words, and nourish an eschatological vision of faith, but without divorcing this from a critical reading of history and of the responsibility Christians have for the here and now. The biblical Apocalypse and an apocalyptic reading of life as practised by the engaged communities 'unite eschatology and politics, myth and praxis, conscience and historical transformation. The Apocalypse is not only vision, catharsis, or protest. History is not only in the hands of God . . .'[9] Even if the brothers and sisters of these communities believe that it may be mainly in God's hands, we too have to act and work. This means that in interpreting history they link faith with politics, avoiding an ingenuous or fanatical hope. The community is called to believe, hope, and act.

These two ways of interpreting the eschatological character of faith exactly mirror the fact that in the Catholic Church there are still some monastic orders or communities which justify their distancing from reality by an eschatological vocation, while others, precisely because of their eschatological vocation, become more engaged, not with the world as such, but in the midst of the People of God.[10]

V. Longing for other apocalypses

I have recently been in contact with the culture of the indigenous people who lived in the region where we have an ecumenical centre. I found once more that the indigenous communities have good cause to enjoy the apocalyptic passages of the Bible so much. They are the pages that are most like the histories and ancestral traditions of the indigenous and black cultures. Knowing this makes pastoral agents more circumspect in dealing with these traditions and these ways of reading the Bible. Like those who tread on the holy ground of meeting God, Mother of Compassion, these brothers and sisters will take off their sandals and walk more humbly on the ground of the hearts and faith of others, able to appreciate that, even with some ambiguities, their spiritual traditions and ways of reading the Bible also reveal 'what the Spirit is today saying to the churches'.

Translated by Paul Burns

Notes

1. P. Freston, 'Evangélicos na Política Brasileira', in *Religiao e Sociedade*, ISER 16/1–2, Nov. 1992, 26.
2. L. Silveira Campos, 'Protestantismo Histórico e Pentecostalismo no Brasil: Aproximaçoes e Conflitos', in *Na Força do Espírito*, 82.
3. S. Takatsu, ibid., 63.
4. T. Scolari, 'Le Pentecôtisme: un état d'Esprit', *L'Actualité Religieuse au Monde* 137, 15 Oct. 1995, 44.
5. G. Gutiérrez, *We Drink from our Own Wells*, Maryknoll and London 1984, 57.
6. V. Codina, 'The Wisdom of Latin America's Base Communities', *Concilium* 1994/4, 75, citing J. Comblin, 'A nova evangelizaçao', in *Sto Domingo: Ensaios Teológico-Pastorais*, Petrópolis 1993, 215.
7. This civilization is not to be confused with the '*colla*' culture of the same region, which flourished around AD 1300, at the time when Pope Boniface VIII instituted the first Roman Jubilee. In 1997 a regional museum was opened in Tiwanaku, housing pre-ceramic fragments dating from 2000 BC and other objects from as late as the Inca period.
8. C. Mesters, *Flor sem Defesa*, Petrópolis 1987, 100 (Eng. Trans. *Defenseless Flower*, Maryknoll, NY 1989).
9. P. Richard, *Apocalípsis, reconstrucción de la esperanza*, San José 1994, 20.
10. Cf. M. Barros, *Na estrada do Evangelo*, Petrópolis 1993.

Millenniarist Messianism in Buddhist History

Aloysius Pieris

Historians freely use the terms millenniarism and messianism to describe certain developments within Asian Buddhism, although initially these notions were associated with a Christian movement which arose out of an exaggeratedly literalistic interpretation of the 'prophecy' in Rev. 20.1–15, that Satan would be bound up for a thousand years and then let loose for a while. The dawn of such a millennium has been interpreted variously by amillenniarists, premillenniarists and postmillenniarists, but always in terms of the 'Time of the Christ or the Messiah'. In other words, the point of reference has always been the dawn of a messianic era either coinciding with or at least orientated towards the end-time. However, in discussing 'millenniarist messianism' in a Buddhist context, we must be aware that notions such as messianic era and end-time lose their specifically Christian overtones.

Buddhism teaches nothing that even approximates to the Christian projection of an end-time or a parousia, the dawn of 'a new heaven and a new earth', the vision of the cosmos transformed with the finality of the risen Christ. Buddhism allows us to speak only of the end-time of one cycle in an endless existence. In this sense, one Buddha-era could be followed by the dawn of a new aeon which might usher in the life and activity of another Buddha.

The Buddhist scriptures also allude to the new era in terms of a span of 1000 years contracted to 500, as will be explained below. In this sense one can trace, among certain Buddhist sects during certain periods of Buddhist history, a 'millenniarist' expectation of an end-time associated with a messianic era. The concept of a millennium can be taken only symbolically as a period of time that might either herald the messianic era, or coincide with it. In any case, every form of millenniarist messianism has been regarded as a deviation from Buddhist orthodoxy.

The cosmic signs announcing the Buddha era

In a passage that has not yet caught the attention of scholars, a Theravadin monk-exegete of the late sixth century CE, writes that when the Buddha-to-be (*Bodhisattva*) was born in his last human existence,

> [. . . .] the blind received their sight; the deaf heard sounds; the dumb spoke; the hunchbacked straightened up; the crippled resumed walking; all captives were released from their chains and fetters.[1]

These pre-signs (*pubba-nimittāni*) of the Buddha-era also include the depletion of purgatories or 'temporal hells' (fortunately, no hell is eternal in Buddhism!), the elimination of fear among the animals, pleasant climatic changes, sweetening of sea water, and, of course, as could be expected in a literature saturated with Buddhist symbolism, the blooming of a variety of lotuses in all places.

These 'miracles', as they are explicitly called,[2] are not mentioned in the canonical references to the birth of the Buddha. This text, written over a millennium later, is a Buddhist 'after-thought' on the significance of the special moment in history when a Great Person (*Mahāvīra*) would appear as the Discoverer of the Path of Deliverance. The text says that the future Buddha was still in the Tusita heaven, when the *devatā* (the 'gods' or the cosmic powers of the universe) appealed that the propitious time had arrived for him to be born as a human person and reach the deathless state, 'causing the [world] together with the gods to cross [the Ocean of Rebecoming] (*sadevakam tārayanto*)'.[3]

Now the technical term *tārayanto* is significant. One is said to be saved when one 'crosses' (*tarati*) the Ocean of Rebecoming. This means, one is saved when one saves oneself; for nobody can cross the ocean on behalf of another. But the idea of 'saving others' (as in the above-quoted passage) is conveyed by the same verb in its causative form: *tārayati* ('making others cross' the Ocean of Rebecoming). Here the Buddha is referred to as 'saving' (*tārayanto*), obviously, in the only sense that Buddhist orthodoxy allows him to be called a Saviour, namely that he offers the opportunity for salvation by discovering and disclosing the ancient 'Noble Path'. It is the Pathfinder's arrival, i.e., the dawn of the Buddhist Era, that is imagined to have been heralded by miraculous cosmic changes.

Although this text occurs only in some of the post-scriptural commentaries, its message can help us to contrast the Buddhist and the biblical understanding of the messianic signs. Knowing this difference, we can situate the Buddhist version of millenniarist messianism in its own proper context.

In Isaiah (34; 35) the Saviour comes with a message of severe judgment against the nations (34) and a message of deliverance to the chosen people (35). The good news of deliverance, the Saviour's arrival and the righteous people's home-coming to Zion, as well as the opening of the Holy Path that is safe and sure, are accompanied by the blind seeing, the deaf hearing, the lame leaping like a deer, the dumb speaking, water springing forth from the desert, grass turning into reeds and the ravenous and frightful beasts disappearing. Salvation in the Hebrew scriptures is not only individual; it is social and cosmic, as are the very signs that anticipate it.

The Christian scriptures interpret this 'prophecy' as having been fulfilled when Jesus came as the Messiah (Matt. 11.4–6), and as 'spilling over' (to borrow a phrase of Moltmann's) to a future appearance of the same Christ. The imminence of the end-time coinciding with the coming of Christ – whether conceived and expressed prophetically or apocalyptically – presupposes the Judaeo-Christian belief in a world created as good, but fallen, and yet redeemed into a new creation, obviously within a unilinear history constituted by an ongoing fulfilment of an ever-renewed promise.[4] The messianic signs, therefore, anticipate the coming new order of total redemption, like little Tabors anticipating the new life of the Crucified One exalted on the cross, drawing all creation into his paschal glory, and gathering all persons into his transfigured body. They express the already of the not yet.

Buddhism, by contrast, denies a creator-redeemer God, and has no doctrinal space for a promise-fulfilment concept of history. *Nirvāna* or the final release from the round of becoming is never equated with a transformed state of the universe, i.e., a 'new heaven and new earth'. Hence these miracles are not the pre-signs (*pubba-nimittāni*) of the radical cosmic transformation of the end-time, as in Christianity. On the contrary, the miraculous changes in nature are mere announcement-signs of the long awaited arrival of the Discoverer of the Salvific Path. Not performed by the Buddha-to-be, they are explained as the joyous momentary response of the cosmos to his long-awaited arrival.[5] A messianism that aimed at similar changes as constitutive of a Buddha era would, therefore, be a departure from Buddhist orthodoxy.

The scriptural basis of millenniarist messianism

Two different scriptural texts have combined to form the basis of a millenniarist messianism among certain Buddhist sects. Each contains a 'prophecy' attributed to the Buddha. The first is recorded in the Book of Discipline. The Buddha is shown to have yielded reluctantly and grudgingly to pressures from his own stepmother, Mahāprajāpatī Gotami, and his beloved disciple, Ānanda, when he established the Order of Nuns, not without canonical precautions that reveal a male mistrust of women.[6] Having established the Women's Order, the Buddha is made to appear to have regretted the action:

> If, Ānanda, women had not obtained the going forth from home into homelessness in the *dhamma* and discipline proclaimed by the Truth-finder, the Brahma-faring, Ānanda, would have lasted long; true *dhamma* would have endured for a thousand years. But, since, Ānanda, women have gone forth . . . in the *dhamma* and discipline proclaimed by the Truth-finder, now, Ānanda, the Brahma-faring will not last long; the true *dhamma* will endure only for a five hundred years.[7]

This whole narrative reveals a strong male editorial hand that has attributed to the Buddha an anti-woman attitude which contradicts the overall image that he projects in the scriptures as a whole.[8] What matters, however, is not the authenticity of the text, but its explosively apocalyptic potential when combined with that other prophecy, also recorded in the scriptures, which describes the social-spiritual crisis that precedes a new Buddha era. The first prophecy has received a millenniarist twist, whereas the second, which we quote below, has yielded to a messianic interpretation. Together they have fed many religio-political movements.

The second prophecy occurs in one of the Long Discourses of the Buddha.[9] There, he predicts a gradual deterioration of religion and society to a point when humans themselves begin to behave like beasts until finally sanity returns to a repentant few. From these few, there would gradually emerge a whole generation of people endowed with virtue, comeliness and longevity. From among them would then arise two universal persons wielding a world-wide authority, the one in the religious sphere (*dhamma-cakka*) and the other in the secular sphere (*ānā-cakka*). The former is the Buddha, whose name significantly would be Metteyya (Pali) or Maitreya (Sanskrit), 'the friendly one' or 'one full of love'. His secular counterpart, Sankha by name, would also conquer and govern the world non-violently (*adaṇḍena asatthena dhammena*),[10] i.e., 'not by the scourge, not by the sword, but by righteousness'.[11] They are each called a *cakka-vatti* (Pali) or *cakra-vartin* (Sanskrit), a phrase that plays on the word *vatti/vartin*, 'one who turns' or 'one who observes one's religious duties'. *Cakra* means a 'wheel' (or 'sphere', as I translate it here). To exploit the full meaning of the pun, we should say that as a turner (*vatti*) of the wheel (*cakka*), they are each dutiful (*vatti*) in their respective 'spheres' (*cakka*) of authority.

A fundamentalist reading of these two 'prophecies' in any given context of religious and social decadence could provoke a millenniarist-messianic movement. Already the Lotus Sutra of Northern Buddhism had elaborated the germinal idea of the three periods of the *dharma*: the period of the True Law, the period of a counterfeit Law and finally the period of decadence of the Law. In China the most prevalent view was that the first period lasted only 500 years and the second 1000 years. Thus there was a millenniarist sect that believed they were in the period of decadence and appealed to a disciplined and austere life.[12]

In Japan, too, the same idea crystallized into a passive form of fideism, a belief in the grace of the Amitabha as in the Jodo Sect, which is said to have given rise to a later combative branch called 'Shin' (by Shinran, 1172–1212). This abolished monasticism and celibacy, and advocated laxity ('wine, women, and meat') as an inevitable option in a period when only grace could save.[13] The popular aggressive nationalism that Nichiren (1228–1282) triggered off with his apocalyptic interpretation of the Lotus Sutra can be cited as another messianic movement,[14] which has re-emerged in a modern garb in today's Soka Gakkai.

Such tendencies can be detected in many Buddhist cultures. Here, we shall concentrate on the most manifest forms of millenniarist messianism as recorded in Buddhist annals of Mynmar (former Burma) and China, as these have merited detailed scholarly studies. I apologize for retaining the old spellings of Burmese and Chinese names as found in the works I cite.

Some examples from Mynmar[15]

The decline of Buddhism under local kings and under Britain's mercantile domination of Mynmar in the nineteenth century had jolted the Buddhists into thinking that they were experiencing the period of economic and spiritual decay 'prophesied' by the Buddha. Burma's territorial and economic losses to the British East India Company during the reign of King Bagyidaw (1819–1837) created the ideal situation for the first Buddhist messianic uprising in that country. The various revolutionary movements seem to have identified the secular and the spiritual 'sphere' (*cakka*) of 'dutiful' (*vatti*) governance in one single person, a sort of 'Buddha-King' who had to rise and bring about a peaceful and prosperous state of affairs. It was hoped that Setkya-min (*cakkavatti*), the Universal Righteous Ruler,[16] would later come as Arimadeya (the Burmanized version of *Maitreya*, the future Buddha).

Thus Bagyidaw's heir apparent who called himself Setkya-min (*Cakkavatti*) was executed by the next king in April 1838, but in the popular legends he was believed to be alive, having been preternaturally saved from death. Rebellions followed one after the other under his name. Already in January 1839 Maung Tsetkya, claiming to be Setkya-Min, started a revolt in Pegu. The very mention of this title drew followers. The uprising was crushed with great difficulty, and the messianic pretender executed in March that year. Similar impersonations of Setkya-Min were repeated several times in the year 1855.

Once Lower Burma was annexed by the British East India Company in 1852, Buddhist messianism, which was earlier directed against the declining local monarchy, became nationalist and anti-Western. In 1858, a local fisherman showed himself up as Buddha Metteyya, born to expel the *Kalas* (Western foreigners); his followers managed to arrest a British Colonial Commissioner. In 1860, another Future Buddha ('Paya:-alaung') became a threat to the British in the town of Toungoo. He was cornered by mobilizing all the locally available troops and eventually hanged by Captain Lloyd. Local songs of the period (1861–1862) refer to a certain messianic prince who had the mission to expel the British.

After the British had conquered the rest of Burma (1885–1886) and deported King Mindon's successor, there began a wave of anti-British resistance which invariably came from persons who claimed to be Buddha-King (*Buddha-Yaza*), Dharma-King (*Dhamma-Yaza*) or Cakkavatti-prince (*Setkya-mintha*). In the period 1886–1887, the British had to face the challenge of a pretender called 'Buddha Yaza Min Laun' (Buddha-King and Future Monarch) in the Yemethin district. Several similar armed rebellions led by men claiming messianic titles such as those given above have been recorded also in the period between 1887–1912.

These 'liberation movements' of various Dhamma-kings had prepared the ground for the independence-struggles of the urban political elite belonging to the General Council of Burmese Associations in the early part of this century. In fact in 1922, the president of one of its provincial associations declared himself anointed as Setkya-min and drew about 20,000 followers against the colonial masters. After his movement was suppressed, a Buddhist hermit called Bandaka appeared in a Cakkavatti's attire claiming to be the restorer of the ideal Buddhist kingdom. Begun in

1924, his movement survived until 1928, when he was captured and sentenced to deportation for life. To this must also be added the ex-monk Saya San's peasant revolt (1930–1932), initiated primarily against money-lenders. The Setkya-min idea was operative here, too. Monks and ex-monks played a vital role in it.[17]

The Chinese version of millenniarist messianism[18]

China, too, saw many Buddhist uprisings from 402 CE onwards, climaxing in 515 in the violent rebellion of Fa-King – a monk who married a nun, preached a 'parousia of a new Buddha', ravaged monasteries, burnt books, and took control over the state-managed church, brandishing the slogan 'A new Buddha has appeared'.

Since then, at least four messianic sects seem to have arisen. The most significant one was the Maitreya sect, founded in 610 CE by a monk who declared himself emperor, and which was active right up to the sixteenth century. Here the main inspiration came from Pure Land Buddhism, fired by the hope of transforming the country into a peaceful Buddha-Land ruled by Holy Rulers reborn from the 'Western paradise' of the Buddha Amitabha. By the Middle Ages there were three more: the White Cloud Sect (1108–1300), and two others which continued up to the twentieth century, namely, the Lo Sect (1505–1956) and the White Lotus Sect (1133–1813), a branch of which (I-Kuam Tao) was hunted out by Chairman Mao Ze Dong in 1956.

Of these, perhaps the White Lotus sect (*Pai Lien Ts'ai*) had been the most effective. It was a shoot of the Amidist Lay Societies founded by Mao Tzu Yuan (1086–1166), an ordained monk and court preacher who aimed at declericalizing Buddhism. His movement was very popular, led by married monks and characterized by women's participation, and very much in conflict with both the orthodox monastic order and the imperial government. There was strict discipline in the movement even with regard to diet (no meat, no wine). The movement was proscribed many times as it organized many rebellions, and Mao Tsu Yuan's successor, who was called Little Mao (Hsiao Mao), was exiled several times. Their most successful armed rebellion took place in 1351. Led by Han Shan T'ung, who called himself Buddha Maitreya, it destroyed the Mongol rule and established a new dynasty under Chu Yuan-Chan, a former Buddhist novice and officer of the White Lotus Army. Ironically, under Confucianist influence, he turned anti-Buddhist, called himself Emperor of the Ming Dynasty and proscribed the White Lotus sect which brought him to power. As mentioned earlier, I Kuam Tao, which was hunted out by Mao Ze Dong in our century, was an offshoot of this messianic sect.

The reason for such movements can be traced back to the political instability experienced since the division of China in 202 CE. I have already mentioned the early Buddhist rebellions from 402 to 515. But the messianic sects mentioned above flourished mostly after the chaotic South Sung period (1127–1179). Over and above the hope in the Buddha's prophecy about the arrival of Maitreya after a period of decadence, and the Amitabha cult of the Buddhists who wished to see the Western Paradise or the Pure Land realized here on earth, there were also non-Buddhist ideals or ideologies that influenced the Buddhist vision of a social utopia. There was, for instance, the Confucian ideal of the Enlightened Emperor. Taoists, too, hoped for the Great Peace to be brought about by the True Ruler (Chen Chun). The Manicheans also spoke of the Ruler of Light (Ming Wang), a title that Han Shan T'ung gave his son. Finally there were also Taoist secret societies (Yellow Turban Society, Five Pecks of Rice Society, etc.) which aimed at establishing an ideal religious state. In fact the White Lotus Society of the Buddhists seems to have borrowed many religious practices and beliefs from such Taoist societies.

The significance for the future

Let us first identify the deviant elements in these movements. The Buddha's 'prophecy' clearly speaks in terms of a dual authority, the one spiritual and the other secular, but their efficacious complementarity is based on the fact that the Dhamma remains their common ground. Thus a dialectical dualism in the guidance and governance of humans remains the Buddhist ideal.[19] But the messianic movements announcing the end of a turbulent period ('millennium'?) and the dawn of peaceful era were characterized by a politico-religious monism: there was just one Cakkavatti and he was both Buddha and King, or at least he claimed to be a spiritual authority with a political mandate. This is a departure from the Buddhist ideal. Furthermore, the means of bringing in the new messianic era was armed insurrection, and this too contradicts the basic teaching of Buddhism. Finally, the enemy to be conquered was not human greed infecting society and creating an unfair social order (as very clearly envisaged in the Buddhist scriptures), but merely the hostile secular leadership of the country.

On the positive side, we see a revolutionary potential in Buddhism, which certainly has a social gospel, too. The scriptures offer a social utopia which is worth the attempt to approximate to in politico-religious terms. The non-Buddhist ideologies played a vital role in these Buddhist attempts. For all religious ideals remain utopian unless an appropriate ideology, i.e., a programmatic vision with a concrete agenda, is made to convert them into a social reality. The collaboration between ideology and religion in generating required social changes – with the not altogether inevitable risk of an ideology gradually swallowing up religion and becoming despotic – has been illustrated in the history of Buddhism and also other Asian religions.[20]

The other positive element is the role of 'cosmic religiosity' in all social transformations in Asia. The cosmic, as opposed to the secular, is our neologism for the sacred this-worldliness of tribal and clan cultures, as well as of the popular religiosity forming the sub-structure of almost all major religions. The source of inspiration in the revolutions recorded above was this popular religiosity in conflict with the institutional centres of the metacosmic religion. In these messianic movements, the class conflict between the lower clergy and the higher clergy becomes evident. The cosmic component – which included the earthly and the feminine – also accounts for the eco-concerns and the women's participation in some of the messianic movements.

Does not this consideration invite Asians to venture into a salutary species of millenniarist messianism? Perhaps the need of the hour is a globalized messianism of a non-fundamentalist sort involving all persons of good will against the globalized cultural and economic invasion which this millennium has ushered in. The latter makes all former threats of colonialism a mere foreshadowing of the Attractive Beast (Rev. 13): the Money Demon or Absolutized Capital, which is about to swallow all that is beautiful and holy not only in Buddhism but in all Asian soteriologies. To conscientize its victims (the Asian poor) that they are the Lamb that is slain, from whom alone liberation can come (Rev. 14), is the new evangelical task of the Asian church. A neo-messianism fed by the finest elements in Asia's revolutionary tradition, Buddhist and non-Buddhist, has to be unleashed against the true enemy of humanity: greed organized into principalities and powers. Such would in fact be the distinctive feature of an Asian theology of liberation. Covenanted with the other religionists, we should exploit our common religious resources for a truly globalized resistance against this global danger. I ardently hope that such a programme of inter-religious collaboration will find its way into the forthcoming Asian Synod's agenda as its all embracing mission for the coming millennium.

Notes

1. Dhammapalācariya, *Udānaṭṭhakathā* (ed. F. L. Woodward), Pali Text Society, London 1977, 149.

2. Ibid., 150.

3. This is a quotation from an earlier commentary, *Dhammapadatnaṭṭhakathā (The Commentary on the Dhammapada*, ed. H. C. Norman, Pali Text Society, London 1970), Vol. 1, 84.

4. Jurgen Moltmann, *Theology of Hope*, London 1967, especially 102–12.

5. In fact, it is said that the blind gained sight (etc.) as if to see the Buddha's splendour which lit up the whole universe: *appamāṇo obhāso phari. Tassa sirim danatthukāmā viya andhā cakkhūni patilabhiṃsu* [*Udānatnaṭṭhakathā*, n. 1 above].

6. *The Book of Discipline* (I. B. Horner's annotated English translation of the *Vinaya Pitaka*), Pali Text Society, London ⁴1988, 352ff.

7. Ibid., 356.

8. See Aloysius Pieris, *Fire and Water. Basic Issues in Asian Buddhism and Christianity*. Maryknoll, NY 1996, 33–4.

9. *Dialogue of the Buddha* (T. W. Rhys David's English Translation of the *Dīgha Nikāya*), Part III, Pali Text Society, Oxford 1991, 59–76.

10. *Dīgha-nikāya* (ed. J. E. Carpenter), Pali Text Society, London 1976, Vol. III, 76.

11. As translated by Rhys Davids in *Dialogue of the Buddha* (see n. 9 above), 73.

12. Kenneth K. S. Ch'en, *Buddhism*, New York 1968, 158–9.

13. Paul Demièville, 'Le Buddhisme et la guerre' [postscript to G. Renondeau 'L'histoire des moines guerriers du Japon'], *Melanges*, Paris 1957, 347–85: 372.

14. Ibid., 372.

15. The primary source of information for this section is E. Sarkisyanz, *Buddhist Backgrounds of the Burmese Revolution*, The Hague 1965, 150–9.

16. The Burmanized version of Cakkavatti is *Setkyawade*; but its messianic version is *Setkya-min*.

17. Sarkisyanz, *Buddhist Backgrounds* (n. 15), 160ff.

18. Daniel L. Overmyer, 'Folk Buddhist Religion: Creation and Eschatology in Medieval China', *History of Religion* XII/1, August 1972, 42–70. This source is complemented here with the information provided by Demièville, 'Le Buddhisme et la guerre' (n. 13).

19. See Aloysius Pieris, 'The *Mahāpurisa* Ideal and the Principle of Dual Authority', *Dialogue* NS XXIII, 1996, 168ff.

20. As shown in my *Fire and Water* (n. 8), ch. 9, esp. 103–12.

In the End – God

Jürgen Moltmann

I. In the end – the new beginning

The question whether the world has an end is a typically apocalyptic question. Some speak of the 'end of all things', others of the 'end of the world' or the 'end of history'. Why do we ask about the end? Can we no longer bear the present state of things? Do the experiences of history torment us so much that, like the Germans at the end of the Second World War, we say, 'Better a horrific end than this endless horror'? Or are we afraid that things which are dear and precious to us will not continue? Can we not get enough of this world, so that its possible end fills us with fear and trembling? Do the economic and ecological crises of the present torment us so much that we are afraid of coming world catastrophes? Any idea of 'the end' is ambivalent: it can fascinate us or terrify us.

In Christian theology, questions about the 'end' are treated as the 'last questions' in eschtology.[1] Eschatology is the doctrine of the 'last things' (*ta eschata*). Hans Urs von Balthasar has called the last part of his 'Theo-Drama' of world history 'The End Game'; in doing so he was certainly thinking of Samuel Beckett.[2] Lastly, the 'final solution' of all unresolved problems in personal life, in human history and in the cosmos is to come. Apocalyptic fantasy has always depicted God's great Last Judgment, on the last day of the world, with great passion. Then the eternal God will speak the last word: the good will go to heaven, the evil to hell, and the earth will be destroyed in a conflagration. The acts of world history are concluded in the judgment of the world. We also know the fantasies of the final battle between Christ and the Antichrist, between God and the devils in the 'Valley of Armageddon', a battle which in the Middle Ages was thought to be decided by fire from heaven, and in modern fundamentalism is thought to be decided by atom and hydrogen bombs, but not before the pious have been miraculously 'raptured', so that only the godless perish in the fire. Before Hiroshima in 1945 fire was the means of the apocalyptic final solution; since then it has been annihilation.[3]

All these notions and ideas are genuinely apocalyptic, but they are not Christian. The Christian expectation of the future has nothing to do with such final solutions, since its focal point is not 'the end of life', history or the world, but rather the beginning: the beginning of eternal life, the beginning of the kingdom of God, and the beginning of the 'world to come', as the Nicene Creed says. It is God's new beginning in the end of temporal life, the form of this world and this temporal creation. The Christian hope expects the beginning in the end. Dietrich Bonhoeffer said good-bye to his fellow prisoners on 9 April 1945, when he was being taken to the place of execution in Flossenbürg concentration camp, with the words, 'It is the end – for me the beginning of life.'[4] Expectations of the end are Christian only when their future horizons develop from the memory of the crucifixion and resurrection of the crucified Christ into the coming glory of God. The end of Christ, too, was and is his true beginning. The Christian expectation of the end does not draw the lines of the past and present development of world history into the future, in order then to make conjectures about a good or usually a bad end. Rather, it sees in the cross of Christ the anticipation of the end of this age of sin, death and the devil, because in the resurrection of Christ it believes in the beginning of the new life and the new creation of all things, and already experiences it in the Spirit.

For the Christian hope, Christ is the promise, the overture and the real beginning of true life in the midst of this false life, the recreation of all transitory things for the eternal creation and the indwelling of God in the alien land of our wildernesses. Therefore here the expectation is not only of the new beginning in the end, but also of the end in the new beginning. If the risen Christ is the pioneer of eternal life, then in him we also recognize the end of this temporal life. If the risen Christ is the life-giving spirit of God, then he overcomes death in the victory of life. Only in him do we recognize the 'world under the cross' with all that is wrong in it, all that is to be destroyed and annihilated, brought to an end and made to disappear. It is not that the 'end of the world' brings God's new beginning, but conversely that God's new beginning brings this perverse world to its merited and longed-for end. We only recognize the darkness of the night in the light of the new day, evil in the good, and the deadliness of death in our love for life. There is nothing intrinsically creative about the annihilation of life or a world. We cannot force in the new creation by the destruction of our world.

The true 'end of the world' is only the side of the beginning of 'God's new world' which is turned towards us. We can also understand the passing away of the old world and the coming of the new, like the resurrection of the crucified and dead Christ, as a process of divine transformation and transfiguration. Nothing will be annihilated, but everything will be changed.[5] So the pains of the decline of this world are something like the birth pangs of God's new world, as Paul imagines them in Rom. 8.18ff.[6] Therefore the answer given by the Christian expectation of the future to apocalyptic questions about 'the end of the world' is the making present in memory of the crucified and risen Christ as the answer. This is the only answer that we can give with the certainty of faith. It is not the answer to all apocalyptic questions about God's righteousness and the future of the dead. In the end Christ himself died with the question, 'My God, why have you forsaken me?' on his lips. But in the community of the crucified Christ and in the hope of the risen Christ we can live with the unanswerable 'last questions' without giving premature answers or sinking without an answer into numbing.

Ideas about the 'end of the history' can be distinguished by whether they are about the goal of history (*telos*) or the end of history (*finis*). If world history has a goal, then this is its consummation and history goes in stages towards this goal. According to the biblical traditions the 'thousand-year kingdom' in which Christ will rule with his people in peace over the nations (Rev. 20 after Dan. 7) is such a goal. After the bestial kingdoms of violence comes the humane kingdom of the Son of man. According to ancient ideas it is 'the golden age' (Virgil), according to modern hope 'the kingdom of freedom' (Mark) or 'of eternal peace' (Kant). For Francis Fukuyama, formerly in the State Department in Washington, in 1989, after the collapse of socialism, capitalism and liberal democracy became 'the end of history'. We call such ideas of the end chiliastic or millenarian. But if world history comes to an end in the end of the world, it is broken off by catastrophes. According to biblical traditions that is the 'destruction of the world', according to ancient notions the 'world conflagration', and according to modern fears a global nuclear annihilation or ecological catastrophe. In modern terminology we call such notions of the end apocalyptic. Their 'end of the world' does not divide the course of world history, but makes nonsense of any era of history. The history of the world is a meaningless history of suffering and its end is the best thing about it.

The modern belief in progress is a secularized form of the

millenarianism of salvation history: modern anxieties about the destruction of the world and dreams of the annihilation of the world are secularizations of the old apocalyptic. Those who have power are interested in the progress of history. They understand the future as a continuation and consummation of their present. Those who are helpless and oppressed are not interested in progress and the consummation of their history of suffering, but only in its rapid and alternative future.[7] We must put to the different notions of goal and end with the question, 'Whom do they benefit?'

II. The goal of world history: 'the thousand-year kingdom'

No hope has fascinated people so much and done so much damage as the idea of the 'thousand-year kingdom'.[8] Christians expected Christ's kingdom of peace, Romans the 'golden age'; modern men and women expect 'the end of history' in a future state which has no history and is free of conflict. The first fulfilment of this hope was offered in the surprising 'Constantinian shift', when persecuted Christianity first became a 'permitted religion' in the Roman empire; subsequently, under the emperors Theodosius and Justinian, it became the dominant and dominating religion of the empire. Those who have suffered with Christ will reign with him (I Cor. 6.2; II Tim. 2.12). So the political shift was interpreted in millenarian terms as the shift from martyrdom to millennium: 'the holy empire' is already Christ's thousand-year kingdom (Rev. 20), in which Christ will rule with his followers and judge the peoples. The saint of the *sacrum imperium* was St George, who kills the dragon, the symbol of the enemies of God and the empire. The guardian angel of the empire was the archangel Michael, who kills the dragon in heaven.

The *imperium sacrum* also begins with a cross. However, it was not in the sign of the cross of Christ on Golgotha but of the cross in his dream that the emperor Constantine triumphed in 312. So the martyr cross of Christ became the victorious cross of the Christian empire. It appears among the military orders and on the banners of Christian nations (the George Cross, the Victoria Cross, the Iron Cross, etc.). When the church of Christ became the imperial church of the Roman empire, it handed over the mission of the gospel and faith to the Christian rulers, who saw their religious mission as converting the peoples through subjecting them to Christ's end-time kingdom of peace. The decisive question was not belief or unbelief, but, 'Baptism or death?' That is how the Saxons and the Slavs in the early Middle Ages and the people of Latin America at the beginning of modern times were missionized.

Another form of the fulfilment of this hope can be found in the epoch-making awareness of the 'new times'.[9] The 'new times' are the third age of humankind which the Italian visionary Joachim of Fiore had prophesied in the twelfth century as the coming 'third age of the Spirit'. The 'new times' are always also the 'last times', since after the 'new age' only the end of the world can come. The conquest of America from 1492 on and the seizure of scientific and technological power over nature was sufficient occasion for understanding the European rule over the world as a messianic fulfilment of world history and justifying it with this solemnity about the 'last age'. The fact that the United States imagines itself as the 'new world'[10] and has 'the new world order' (*novus ordo seculorum*) on its seal accords with the European ideas of a 'Christian age' and the 'new age'. In Europe the 'utopian age' of the social utopias and the legal utopias begins with the American Declaration of Independence and the French Revolution of 1789: 'All human beings are born free and equal.' The declarations of human rights and the establishment of individual civil rights in various states on the basis of universal civic rights on the one hand, and the notions of a 'classless society' in the socialist worker movements on the other, left their mark on the spirit of the nineteenth century. But the conflict between rights to freedom and equal claims remained. In both movements – the democratic and the social movements – Europe attempted to justify its rule over the world by the universalism of humankind and a humane state. The particular values of the Western world were offered to all peoples and all men and women as the universal values of the modern world.

The most recent prophet of the Western 'end of history' has been Francis Fukuyama.[11] A follower of the quite remarkable interpretation of Hegel by the Russian philosopher Alexandre Kojève in Paris, he saw the collapse of socialism in the Soviet empire as the dawn of the 'end of history'. The triumph of the West lies in the fact that since 1989 there has been no real alternative to capitalism and liberal democracy. Similar forms of democratic state will develop everywhere. The common satisfaction of material needs will be provided for by 'the global marketing of everything'. We stand at the end of the great conflicts between different political and economic systems and the beginning of a 'world without alternatives'. In pluralistic capitalistic democracy, human beings have finally discovered what they were looking for in all their experiments. Fukuyama's 'end of history' is not a golden age but a 'sorry time' of boredom. A history which was once alive and full of conflict can now only be admired in a museum of history.[12]

The theo-political dream of the thousand-year kingdom of peace in which Christ and his followers will rule and judge the people was an impossible dream. The external and even more the internal crises of the Holy Roman Empire led to deep disappointments and apocalyptic anxieties. The world-political dream of the 'new world' and the 'new time', of human rights and human dignity for every man and woman, was contradicted in the two European world wars of the twentieth century. 'Auschwitz' and 'Hiroshima' are the names for the end of this messianic dream of the modern world. Finally Fukuyama's 'end of history' will also prove to be a bad dream. The protests of humiliated men and women and a violated earth will not allow the state of the world to remain as it is. According to Hegel it is not a lack of an alternative but freedom from contradiction which is the sign of the end of history. And Fukuyama's 'modern world' itself produces those contradictions by which it will perish, or alternatively another world will come into being in its place. These are social and ecological contradictions. The 'free market economy' produces them, but cannot do away with them.

The lesson that we learn from the failure of the dreams of the end of history – whether in the 'thousand-year kingdom of Christ' or the 'global marketing of everything' – is simple: it is impossible to consummate history in history.

III. The end of the world: apocalypse without hope

The fear of a catastrophic end of the world is only the other side of the hope for its glorious consummation. When that hope fails, usually only the fear is left. In the biblical traditions, alongside the prophetic hopes there were always also the apocalyptic prophecies.[13] There are notions of a coming 'downfall of the world' in Isaiah 24–27; Zechariah 12–14; Daniel 2 and 7; and Joel 3. In the New Testament there is the 'Little Synoptic Apocalypse' in Mark 13 par. and the Revelation of John. We speak of apocalypses when the prophecies of the prophets go beyond the history of Israel and assume world-political or cosmic dimensions. Then a 'new world age' or a 'new creation' is promised, in which this 'old world age' or this 'old world' is to find its end. According to Daniel 2 the great human kingdoms of the world will be destroyed, but then 'the God of heaven will establish a kingdom which is eternal and remains indestructible'. According to Daniel 7 that is the human kingdom of the divine 'Son of man'. According to the apocryphal book of Enoch (1.7), 'this earth will be completely destroyed and all that is on it will perish; and judgment will take place upon all'. After that 'the throne of God will become visible', and 'Son of man will come', and heaven and earth will be 'created anew' (45.4).

The biblical apocalypses with their threat of the destruction of the world go back to the saga of Noah and the flood in Gen. 6–9, according to which God destroys human beings and the earth because of the wickedness of the powerful, but then makes his new covenant with the righteous Noah, who is saved from the destruction. In this new covenant it is promised that the world will not be destroyed again (Gen. 9.11). But underlying the biblical notion of the destruction of the world is the deeper anxiety that God might 'repent' of having ever made human beings on this earth and could have withdrawn his resolve about creation altogether. A God who 'judges' the wickedness of the world is interested in it; but a God who turns away from it completely allows the world to sink into chaos and nothingness. The judgment is an expression of hope; it is the destruction that is hopeless.

In contrast to the apocalyptic traditions in the Bible, the catastrophes brought about by human beings are called 'apocalypse now': the nuclear apocalypse, the ecological apocalypse, etc. These interpretations are false because they burden God with something that is the responsibility of human beings. There is no 'nuclear Armageddon'. Human beings have to take responsibility for any nuclear annihilation of humankind, whereas the apocalyptic Armageddon (Rev. 16.16) is God's action. Therefore the latter is full of hope, whereas the former is totally hopeless. The self-annihilation of humankind and the annihilation of the biosphere of this earth by human beings are human crimes and carry no divine revelation, as do the apocalypses of the Bible.

It is not surprising that today the apocalyptic interpretation of the threat of crimes against humanity is giving rise to a new apocalyptic terrorism. It is not far from a passive expectation of the end to an active ending of this world. 'There can be no construction without destruction' was Mao tse Tung's command to the Cultural Revolution in China. It cost the lives of millions of people and laid the best cultural monuments of China in ruins. The mass murderer Pol Pot took Mao's slogan seriously in Cambodia. His Khmer Rouge murdered the older generation in order to be able to build up a 'new world' with the younger generation. They left behind two million dead in the killing fields and a devastated land. Apocalyptic terrorism can lead to mass suicide of the members of sects: in 1978 in Jonestown, Guyana, these were 912 members of a People's Temple sect; in 1993 in Waco, Texas, 78 members of the

Davidian sect, and in Vietnam 52 adherents of a Vietnamese sect expecting the end of the world; in 1994, 53 members of the Solar Temple sect in Canada and Switzerland; in 1997, 39 members of a UFO death cult in San Diego, California. Their motive was a redemptive 'rapture' from this world which is going under, into another, better world. But apocalyptic terrorism can also lead to the mass murder of others for the sake of a better future. Genghis Khan felt that he had been called to mass murder as 'God's vengeance'. The Oklahoma Bomber and the American Militiamen have the same belief. The poison gas sect of Shoko Asahara, which is now on trial in Tokyo, evidently felt itself called to this final apocalyptic struggle.

The biblical apocalypses are not pessimistic scenarios for the destruction of the world which seek to disseminate anxiety and terror and to paralyse people; they hold fast to the hope of God's faithfulness to his creation in the terrors of this age. 'When all this begins to take place, then lift up your heads, for your redemption is near,' promises Luke (21.18). Prophetic hope is hope in action, apocalyptic hope is hope in danger, a hope which is capable of suffering, patient and persistent: whatever may come, in the end there is God. It is a doctrine of hope and has nothing to do with the fantasies about the destruction of the world current among modern prophets and terrorists.

IV. In the end – God's new creation

According to the biblical traditions, world history does not begin with the Fall and therefore it does not end with the destruction of the world either. It begins with the original blessing of the temporal creation and ends with the bliss of the eternal creation. God's last word is not a judgment, but the word of creation: 'Behold, I make all things new' (Rev. 21.5). That is the 'new heaven and the new earth' which are to come when 'the first heaven and the first earth' pass away (Rev. 21.1). All that can be imagined as the judgment or destruction of the world is provisional by comparison with the finality of the new creation.

How are we to imagine this 'new creation'? It is not another creation which takes the place of this world which we know; however, this creation that we know will become radically different. Revelation does not say, 'Behold, I create (Hebrew *bara*) a new thing', but, 'Behold, I make (Hebrew *asa*) all things new.' What has already been created is 'made' new. What becomes different? First of all the relation to God becomes different: the Creator who has created his work comes to his dwelling place and his rest in his creation. His 'indwelling' (*shekhinah*) comes about in heaven and earth and makes both worlds new, by making them the cosmic temple of God. God's glory then dwells in all things and illuminates and transfigures all creatures.[14]

From the notion of God's cosmic indwelling there follows the notion of the transformation of the temporal and mortal creation to an eternal and immortal creation. Whatever has a share in God's glory becomes eternal and immortal like God himself. The creation itself is not destroyed, but only its sinful, temporal, and mortal form. Creation being itself will be transfigured or – as Orthodox theology says – 'divinized', for finite being then will have a share in the infinite being of the indwelling God. The great eschatological process of transformation is the transition from contradictions to correspondences, from temporality to eternity, and from mortality to the immortality of the 'life of the world to come'. Because the righteousness of God is the basis for an eternal world which accords with him, it must first of all be established in the world judgment on all. Therefore in the Christian expectation the judgment of the world is preceded by the new creation of all things. However, that righteousness of God is not retributive penal justice but righteousness which gives the victims and perpetrators of the human history of the world their due. God does not come to judge but to raise up and justify. In this sense we say, 'In the end – God'.

Translated by John Bowden

Notes

1. J. Moltmann, *The Coming of God. Christian Eschatology*, London and Minneapolis 1996.

2. H. Urs von Balthasar, *Theo-Drama. Theological Dramatic History*, Vol. 4, *The End Game*, San Francisco 1966; cf. also M. Kehl, *Eschatologie*, Würzburg 1986; H. Vorgrimler, *Hoffnung als Vollendung*, Freiburg 1980.

3. L. Reinisch (ed.), *Das Spiel mit der Apokalypse. Über die letzten Tage der Menschheit*, Freiburg 1984.

4. E. Bethge, *Dietrich Bonhoeffer*, London and New York 1970, 830.

5. *Vita mutatur, not tollitur*, as the Catholic Preface for the Dead has it.

6. E. Käsemann, *Commentary on Romans*, Grand Rapids and London ²1980, 229ff.

7. See the article by Marcelo Barros, 'The Birth Pains of the Kingdom of God', in this issue.

8. N. Cohn, *The Pursuit of the Millennium*, London 1959; W. Nigg, *Das ewige Reich. Geschichte einer Hoffnung*, Zurich 1944; M. D. Bryant and D. W. Dayton, *The Coming Kingdom. Essays in American Millennialism and Eschatology*, New York 1983; Moltmann, *The Coming of God* (n. 1), 184ff.

9. Here Moltmann is making a play on words which is virtually impossible to render into English: 'Neuzeit' in German is really 'modernity', but unless it is translated 'new times' to indicate the two elements of which it is made up, the connection with 'new world' and 'new world order' does not work [Tr.]. For the whole question see J. Taubes, *Abendländische Eschatologie* (1947), Munich 1991.

10. E. Lee Tuveson, *Redeemer Nation. The Idea of America's Milennial Role*, Chicago 1968.

11. F. Fukuyama, *The End of History*, Harmondsworth 1993.

12. Recently S. P. Huntington has restored the well-known apocalyptic dualism to American politics in his *The Clash of Civilizations*, New York and London 1997.

13. G. M. Martin, *Weltuntergang. Gefahr und Sinn apokalyptischer Visionen*, Stuttgart 1984; U. H. J. Körtner, *Weltangst und Weltende. Eine theologische Interpretation der Apokalyptik*, Göttingen 1988. For the new feminist theology see Catherine Keller, *Apocalypse Now and Then. A Feminist Guide to the End of the World*, Boston 1996.

14. For more detail see Moltmann, *The Coming of God* (n. 10), III.11, 'The Restoration of All Things', 235–56, and IV.5, 'The Cosmic Temple: The Heavenly Jerusalem', 308–20. For exegesis see R. Bauckham, *The Theology of the Book of Revelation*, Cambridge 1993; E. Schüssler Fiorenza, *The Book of Revelation. Justice and Judgment*, Philadelphia 1984.

Contributors

MICHAEL WILLIAMS is Research Fellow at Trinity and All Saints' College, University of Leeds. Ordained for the Archdiocese of Birmingham in 1947 and Doctor of Theology of the Gregorian University in 1950, he has taught theology in Portugal and Britain. His publications include histories of the English seminaries in Rome and Spain and articles in the *New Catholic Encyclopedia* on eschatology. He has served on Catholic juries at the International Film Festivals in Berlin, Venice, San Sabastian and Troia.

Address: 8 Westbrook Lane, Horsforth, Leeds LS18 5RG, UK.

KARL-JOSEF KUSCHEL was born in 1948. He studied German and theology at the universities of Bochum and Tübingen. He did his doctoral studies in Tübingen, where he was an academic assistant, and from 1981 to 1995 worked at the Institute for Ecumenical Research and Catholic Faculty there. He is now Professor of Culture and Inter-Religious Dialogue in the University of Tübingen. As well as editing many works, he has written *Jesus in der deutschsprächigen Gegenwartsliteratur* (1978); *Heute noch knien? Über ein Bild von Edouard Manet* (1979); *Stellvertreter Christi? Der Papst in der zeitgenössischen Literatur* (1980); *Gottesbilder-Menschenbilder. Blicke durch die Literatur unserer Zeit* (1985); *Weil wir uns auf dieser Erde nicht ganz zu Hause fühlen. Zwölf Schriftsteller über Religion und Literatur* (1985); *Born Before all Time: The Dispute over Christ's Origin* (1992); *Laughter: A Theological Reflection* (1994); *Abraham: A Symbol of Hope for Jesus, Christians and Muslims* (1995); *Im Spiegel der Dichter* (1997); *Von Streit zum Wettstreit der Religionen. Lessing und die Herausfurderung des Islam* (1998).

Address: Sandäckerstrasse 2, 72070 Tübingen, Germany.

TERESA OKURE, SHCJ is Professor of New Testament at the Catholic Higher Institute of West Africa (CIWA). Formerly the Academic Dean of CIWA and Executive Secretary of EATWOT, she serves currently on the Executive Committee of the International Association for Mission Studies. Her many articles and chapters in books include 'A New Testament Perspective on Evangelization and Human Promotion', *Journal of Inculturation Theology* 1/2, 1994, 126–43; 'The Mother of Jesus in the New Testament: Implications for Women in Mission', ibid., 2/2, 1995, 196–210; 'Reading from This Place: Some Problems and Prospects', in *Reading from This Place. Vol. 2: Social Location and Biblical Interpretation in Global Perspective*, ed. F. F. Segovia and Mary Ann Tolbert, Minneapolis 1995, 52–66. She is author of *The Johannine Approach to Mission: A Contextual Study of John 4.1–42*, WUNT 2/3, Tübingen 1988, and a commentary on John's Gospel for the *International Catholic Bible Commentary*, to be published in September 1998.

Address: Catholic Institute of West Africa, PO Box 499, Port Harcourt, Nigeria.

HÅKAN ULFGARD was born in Lund, Sweden in 1953. He gained his doctorate of theology in New Testament Exegesis at the Faculty of Theology in the University of Lund in 1989, and from 1990 to 1993 was substituting and external lecturer in New Testament Exegesis at the Faculty of Theology, University of Copenhagen. Since 1993 he has been Assistant Professor in Biblical Exegesis at the Faculty of Theology, University of Lund. His main non-Swedish publications are: *Feast and Future. Revelation 7:9–17 and the Feast of Tabernacles,* CB NTS 22, Lund 1989; 'Le mouvement de Qumrân et le christianisme primitif', *Études* 381, no. 6, 1994, 637–48; 'The Teacher of Righteousness. The History of the Qumran Community and Our Understanding of the Jesus Movement. Texts, Theories and Trajectories', in the Copenhagen Qumran Volume (forthcoming); and *The Story of Sukkot. The Setting, Shaping and Sequel of the Biblical Feast of Tabernacles* (forthcoming).

Address: Dept. of Biblical Studies, University of Lund, Alihelgona Kyrkogata 8, S-223 62 Lund, Sweden.

LEWIS AYRES is Lecturer in Christian Doctrine at Trinity College, Dublin. He studied Classics at St Andrews in Scotland and Theology at Oxford, writing a DPhil on *Anthropology and Ontology in Augustine's* De trinitate (1994). He is the author of *The Trinity: Classical and Contemporary Readings*, Oxford and Cambridge MA, 1998 and *Augustine's Trinitarian Theology*, Washington, DC (forthcoming). He is co-editor of *Christian Origins: Theology, Rhetoric and Community*, London and New York 1998, and of the monograph series Challenges in Contemporary Theology.

Address: University of Dublin, School of Hebrew, Biblical and Theological Studies, Trinity College, Dublin 2, Ireland.

DAMIAN THOMPSON is a journalist and author based in London. Born in 1962, he read Modern History at Oxford University and was the religious affairs correspondent of the *Daily Telegraph* from 1990 to 1994. He is author of *The End of Time: Faith and Fear in the Shadow of the Millennium* (1996), a study of apocalyptic belief which has been translated into six languages. He writes regularly for the *Telegraph* magazine and *The Literary Review* and is studying for a PhD in the sociology of religion at the London School of Economics.

Address: Garden Flat, 27 Pembridge Square, London W2 4DS, England.

KENNETH J. HSU studied geology at Chinese National University, Nanjing and gained his PhD at UCLA in 1953. Between 1953 and 1963 he was a research scientist for Shell Development Co.; he taught in the USA between 1963 and 1967, and between 1967 and 1994 was Professor of Experimental Geology, ETH Zurich. He was editor of *Sedimentology*, 1971–78; President of the International Association of Sedimentologists, 1978–82; Chairman of the International Marine Geology Commission, 1980–89; a member of the Executive Committee, Scientific Commission on Ocean Research; and a member on committees of the Joint Oceanographic Institutes of Deep Earth Sampling, 1969–1988. He was Swiss delegate to UNESCO, 1989–1992; IUGS delegate to ICSU's IBBP/Global Change programme 1988–1992; and an Expert Panel Member, London Dumping Convention, United Nations, 1987–89. He is an honorary fellow of the Geological Society of America, 1979; a foreign associate of the National Academy of Science and a Wollaston Medallist of the Geological Society of London. He is author of 15 books and 400 journal articles.

Address: Institute of Resource and Environmental Geosciences, Colorado School of Mines, Golden, Colorado 80401–1887 USA.

ANDREAS ALBRECHT is Reader in Theoretical Physics at Imperial College, London University. His wide range of interests include cosmology, particle physics and the foundations of quantum mechanics and statistical physics. He is particularly excited by the opportunities for progress which are present in the field of cosmology, due to the rapid increase in the available data expected over the next decade.

CHRIS ISHAM is Professor of Theoretical Physics at Imperial College, London. Most of his research for the last twenty-five years has been in the field of quantum gravity, with particular emphasis on the mathematical and conceptual issues that arise. His main interests outside theoretical physics and mathematics are general philosophy, the work of C. G. Jung, and theology; for four years he served as the chairman of the Science and Religion Forum.

Address: a. albrecht @ ic.ac.uk/c. isham @ ic.ac.uk, The Blackett Laboratory, Imperial College of Science, Technology and Medicine, South Kensington, London SW7 2BZ, England.

STEPHEN O'LEARY is Associate Professor in the Annenberg School for Communication, University of Southern California. He took his undergraduate degree in Comparative Religion at Harvard University, and his PhD in Communication Studies at Northwestern. He is the author of *Arguing the Apocalypse: A Theory of Millennial Rhetoric*, Oxford 1994, and *A Prescription for Millennium Fever*, Oxford 1998.

Address: Annenberg School of Communication, University of Southern California, Los Angeles, CA 90089–0281, USA

MARCELO BARROS is a Benedictine monk. He is fifty-three and is prior of the Monastery of the Annunciation, an ecumenical monastic community involved with workers and those who have been marginalized in society. Since 1977 he has been advisor to the Brazilian Pastoral Land Commission on matters of theology and spirituality. He is a member of EATWOT, and in 1979 with Carlos Mesters founded the Ecumenical Bible Study Centre. He is also one of the advisors to the Assembly of the People of Brazil. His work especially involves relations between the church and Afro-Brazilian culture and spirituality. He has written about twenty books, some about a theology of the earth; others about ecumenical spirituality, liturgy and liturgical inculturation. They include *A Danca do Novo Tempo* (1997) and a novel *A Secreta Magia do Caminho* (also 1997).

Address: Caixa Postal 5, Goiàs GO 7600–000, Brazil.

ALOYSIUS PIERIS is a Sri Lankan Jesuit priest (born 1934); founder-director of the Tulana Research Centre, Kelaniya; editor of *Dialogue*, an international review for Buddhists and Christians; and professor at the Jesuit Centre for Integrated Religious Studies in Kandy. By training he is an Indologist specialized in Buddhology and author of many research studies in medieval exegetical and philosophical writings of the Pali school. Among his theological writings are *An Asian Theology of Liberation* (1988); *Love Meets Wisdom* (1988), and *Fire and Water* (1996). He held the Franciscan Chair of Mission Studies at the Washington Theological Union (1987), and was the Henry Luce Professor of World Christianity in Union Theological Seminary, New York (1988) and A. P. Wilson Distinguished Professor of Theology at the Divinity School, Vanderbilt University, Nashville (1992).

Address: Tulana, Kohalwila Road, Gonawala-Kelaniya, Sri Lanka.

JÜRGEN MOLTMANN was born in Hamburg in 1926 and is a member of the Evangelical-Reformed Church of Germany. He studied at Göttingen, and then was Professor at the Kirchliche Hochschule, Wuppertal from 1958 to 1963, Professor of Systematic Theology at the University of Bonn from 1963 to 1967, and until his recent retirement Professor of Systematic Theology in the University of Tübingen. Among his many works are his famous trilogy *Theology of Hope* (1967), *The Crucified God* (1974) and *The Church in the Power of the Spirit* (1992), and his newly completed systematic theology: *The Trinity and the Kingdom of God* (1981), *God in Creation* (1985), *The Way of Jesus Christ* (1989), *The Spirit of Life* (1992) and *The Coming of God* (1996).

Address: Universität Tübingen, Evangelisch-Theologisches Seminar, Liebermeisterstrasse 12, D 72076 Tübingen, Germany.

The Concilium Foundation announces with regret the death on 23 April 1998 of Mademoiselle Monique Cadic, after a long illness. Mademoiselle Cadic was and her publishing house, Beauchesne Éditeur, have been the publishers of Concilium in the French language since 1974. All who knew her will treasure the memory of her dynamism and her *joie de vivre*.

The editors wish to thank the great number of colleagues who contributed in a most helpful way to the Final Project.

W. Beuken	Leuven	Belgium
K. Derksen	Utrecht	Netherlands
V. Elizondo	Texas	USA
R. Gibellini	Brescia	Italy
H. Häring	Nijmegen	Netherlands
E. A. Johnson	Bronx	USA
B. Kern	Mainz	Germany
S. McEvenue	Montreal	Canada
N. Mette	Münster	Germany
D. N. Power	Washington	USA
J. Riches	Glasgow	Scotland
L. Sowle-Cahill	Chestnut Hill	USA
C. Theobald	Paris	France
M. Vidal	Madrid	Spain
J. Walsh	Botswana	Africa

CONCILIUM

The Theological Journal of the 1990s

Now available from Orbis Books

Founded in 1965 and published five times a year, *Concilium* is a world-wide journal of theology. Its editors and essayists encompass a veritable 'who's who' of theological scholars. Not only the greatest names in Catholic theology, but also exciting new voices from every part of the world, have written for this unique journal.

Concilium exists to promote theological discussion in the spirit of Vatican II, out of which it was born. It is a catholic journal in the widest sense: rooted firmly in the Catholic heritage, open to other Christian traditions and the world's faiths. Each issue of *Concilium* focusses on a theme of crucial importance and the widest possible concern for our time. With contributions from Asia, Africa, North and South America and Europe, *Concilium* truly reflects the multiple facets of the world church.

Now available from Orbis Books, *Concilium* will continue to focus theological debate and to challenge scholars and students alike.

Concilium Subscription Information - outside North America

Individual Annual Subscription (five issues): £25.00

Institution Annual Subscription (five issues): £35.00

Airmail subscriptions: add £10.00

Individual issues: £8.95 each

New subscribers please return this form:
for a two-year subscription, double the appropriate rate

(for individuals)   £25.00   (1/2 years)   . . . .

(for institutions)   £35.00   (1/2 years)   . . . .

Airmail postage
outside Europe +£10.00   (1/2 years)   . . . .

Total . . . .

I wish to subscribe for one/two years as an individual/institution
(delete as appropriate)

Name/Institution . . . .

Address . . . .

. . . .

. . . .

I enclose a cheque for . . . . payable to SCM Press Ltd

Please charge my Access/Visa/Mastercard no. . . . .

Signature . . . . Expiry Date . . . .

Please return this form to:
SCM PRESS LTD 9 - 17 St Albans Place London N1 0NX